Views from the Steel Plant

VOICES AND PHOTOGRAPHS FROM
100 YEARS OF MAKING STEEL
IN CAPE BRETON ISLAND

"People may have forgotten, but we
really had steelworkers here."—Jimmy Hines

"It brought us joy and brought us tears.
It's been here over sixty years.
It built our homes and stilled our fears
And made this island what it is."
—Charlie MacKinnon

EXIT 6

Sydney

Steel Center
of
Eastern Canada

Views from the Steel Plant

VOICES AND PHOTOGRAPHS FROM
100 YEARS OF MAKING STEEL
IN CAPE BRETON ISLAND

Ronald Caplan

WITH 92 PHOTOGRAPHS

Breton Books

Production: Bonnie Thompson, Glenda Watt, and Fader Communications

Over the years, we have received generous help from people knowledgeable about the Steel Plant, and from keepers of documents and photographs, including Cliff Roach and Harvey MacLeod, Sydney Steel Corporation; Larry Boner, N.S. Communications and Information Centre, Still Photo Division; the Staff of the Beaton Institute, Cape Breton University, Sydney, the Abbass Studio Collection, and the Public Archives of Nova Scotia, Halifax. Photos of troops in Sydney, 1923, appeared in Capt. L. W. Bentley's article, "Aid of the Civil Power: Social & Political Aspects 1904-1924," *Canadian Defence Quarterly*, Summer 1978. Dr. Don MacGillivray gave significant guidance regarding the 1923 strike. See his "Aid to the Civil Power: The Cape Breton Experience in the 1920's" in *Acadiensis*, 1974. Ian MacNeil, then editor of the *Cape Breton Post*, gave permission to quote from the *Sydney Post*. Thanks to Sandra Dunn of the Whitney Pier Historical Society (www.whitneypiermuseum.org) and to Carole Lee Boutilier of the Sydney Steel Museum Committee (www.sydneysteelmuseum.com) who each provided rare photographs from the respective collections.

Dr. Don MacGillivray's original article, "Work Poetry / Poésie de Travail: The Industrial Verse of 'Slim' McInnis," appeared in *Labour / Le Travail*, 28 (Fall 1991).

The chapters on women's work in the Steel Plant were edited from interviews by Florence Smith, New Waterford (for Dr. Brian Joseph's "Women in Hard Hats" research project at Cape Breton University), and by *Cape Breton's Magazine*. Photo on page 127 courtesy Kit Falconer, and on page 132 courtesy Mrs. R. A. Shelley (Minnie Paruch).

The brief chronology of the Steel Plant was created from several lists of events, especially from the Steel Plant Museum Committee (provided by Sydney Slaven) and from Michael Earle's chronology prepared for The Steel Project.

All other research, interviews and photography are by Ronald Caplan, edited from articles in *Cape Breton's Magazine*.

Canada Council   Conseil des Arts
for the Arts   du Canada
We acknowledge the support of the
Canada Council for the Arts for our publishing program.

We also acknowledge support from Cultural Affairs,   NOVA SCOTIA
Nova Scotia Department of Tourism, Culture and Heritage. Tourism, Culture and Heritage

We acknowledge the financial support of the Government of Canada
through the Book Publishing Industry Development Program (BPIDP)
for our publishing activities. Canadä

Library and Archives Canada Cataloguing in Publication

Caplan, Ronald, 1942-

Views from the steel plant : voices and photographs from 100 years of making steel in Cape Breton Island / Ronald Caplan.

ISBN 1-895415-69-1

1. Steel industry and trade—Nova Scotia—Sydney—History. 2. Iron and steel workers—Nova Scotia—Sydney—History. I. Title.

HD9524.C23C35 2005   672'.09716'95   C2005-902990-0

Printed in Canada

CONTENTS

CHAPTER 1

Frank Murphy:
The Steel Plant Was Family

We visited Frank Murphy during the last days of the Blast Furnace and the Open Hearth—the last days of the old method of making steel at the Sydney Steel Plant. The new electric arc furnace was just taking over. The last heat in the Open Hearth Furnace was on June 17, 1989, and the last cast from the Blast Furnace was July 2, 1989.

Frank began by reading from his notebook: "The first heat tapped on the Sydney Steel Plant on December 31, 1901.... And the first million tons was tapped on December 28, 1969, at 2:25 Sunday morning...."

FRANK MURPHY: And the first time we ever made 17 heats in 24 hours—that was on March 31, 1969. On the big furnaces. And that was an all-time record. (*And a heat is what?*) Is 200 tons of steel—200 to 250 tons. So it was 3578 tons in one day.

That's why it kills me to see this place go down the drain. And I think today, what they should do is put a crepe on Number 1 Gate and call her dead. That's my feelings of Sydney Steel. It's the end of a complete era—our island is gone. We'll never get over this. To me, now, this is like, cut the head off a turkey and—it's over. Because—as much as I hate to say it—I have no faith in that new electric furnace. The BOF [basic oxygen furnace]. Who knows? I hope I'm wrong.

(*But you worked with an electric furnace before.*) I worked 25 years on one. They built it in 1937. And I worked right on that from 1937 up to 1953. And then I went back on it again, you know, on different times. In fact, I worked on it about 1960.

(*And can you remember your reaction to the company bringing in an electric furnace in 1937?*) Oh, we thought it was fantastic. You know? Because [then] it was only a 10-ton furnace—it was a specialty furnace, for making gun barrels and gun breeches, gun blocks, propeller shafts for the Navy. See, we'd pour a shaft, and in one ingot it would be taken to Trenton and machined down—be forged and machined—be probably 100 to 150 feet long. Just one piece of steel.

That electric furnace—that's where your specialty steel was made: chrome, nickel, titanium—all those. It was a special furnace for alloys.

We were refining right down to the finest thing. We were making all the special axles for the CPR and CNR [Canadian Pacific and Canadian National Railways]. And we were making wire rope used for the pits, for the cables. As I said, we made gun barrels, gun blocks. We even made steel at one time for bobby pins. And steel wool. Now, you imagine going into a store and picking up a little package of steel wool—we used to make that in 200-ton lots. Co-ordinate the steel for it, and we'd send the steel away. We made the steel to make the steel wool.

That was our trouble—we were shipping our raw materials out. Instead of having our factories here [in Cape Breton], we were shipping our raw material away for somebody else to finish it. (*Was that*

2

Frank Murphy: The Steel Plant Was Family

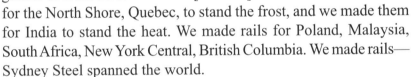

Above: Open Hearth. Right: Frank Murphy's first shift at the Steel Plant—photographed by his mother.

good or bad?) Oh, that was bad, because we lost all the industry. We were just making the rough material. We'd make it and ship it away.

At one time, we made about 200 different grades of steel here. We made [railroad] rails for the North Shore, Quebec, to stand the frost, and we made them for India to stand the heat. We made rails for Poland, Malaysia, South Africa, New York Central, British Columbia. We made rails— Sydney Steel spanned the world.

(*These different places would each require a little different kind of steel.*) Every one of them. Had to make them to their specifications, whatever they wanted. And we made them all here just as—like a woman making a pot of soup. Make your additions and everything else.

And we were using tungsten, which only melts at 3200 degrees. So, you can imagine the heat we'd have in a furnace to melt at 3200. We had to be using nickel and copper, chrome. We made steel here for the bottom of warships—the lowest carbon you could possibly make. It was just like sponge—it would stop a torpedo. It wouldn't explode. Like, if it was 35- or 40-carbon, you hit it, it would shatter. What we made was like a piece of dough—it would go in, and just leave a bulge in it.

All this stuff was made here.

The sad part of this: our story never got out to the world, what we

3

did here. You know? We were owned by an English firm, let's face it. And if they didn't show a profit of 18 to 20 cents on the dollar, 50 years ago, they weren't staying. I always say, we were like Cuba—pardon the expression. We had outside ownership, see. The Americans owned Cuba. They ran it, they put whoever they wanted there. Until Castro overthrew them, and then they got clear of this American ownership. And we had British Empire Steel. All the board of directors never sit here, they always sit in Montreal, and told us what we're going to do down here. This is what killed us.

And then we got into the government. [The Nova Scotia government took over Sydney Steel after the 1967 "Parade of Concern." See Chapter 10.] And that was worse again. Because all the political hacks got jobs. We had fellows out there who didn't know their.... They were just out there—they were friends of a party, and they got a job. The board of directors, now, for Sydney Steel—there's not one steelworker on it.

How can you run a steel plant when you haven't got steel men? You have to have men that know steel to be able to run a steel plant. [There was a fellow there,] he was an engineer of some kind, but he never ran an open hearth furnace. I don't believe he was ever in the Open Hearth. He was never in the Blast Furnace. How the hell could you run a job when you don't know what's going on?

It's great to read a book. Technology is wonderful. I've got a stack of steel books out there. One of them: *Steelmaking for the World Over*. I read it cover to cover, but it didn't tell me how to run an open hearth furnace that was in trouble and it wasn't getting its gas or its oil or the steam, and I'd have to get out and find out what am I going to adjust to bring this heat into control. This book didn't tell me anything about that.

So the war comes. The Japanese are defeated. The Germans are defeated. And what do they do? Germany built up—Germany is stronger than ever they were. They built up Japan—that's cutting their throat today. With steelmaking. Shipping it in there—they're paying five, six, seven dollars an hour. And what's happening? The Americans are buying it.

Now, R. B. Cameron, when he came here, he was here a year or two [after Hawker-Siddeley pulled out and the provincial gov-

4

ernment took over]. We made a million tons of steel in one year [1969]. We burned the Steel Plant down doing it. Took it to the core. And what did R.B. do? He takes our Nail Mill to Dartmouth. He bought it from the government. And he's buying his steel from Germany—offshore steel—to make his nails up there in Dartmouth. He didn't buy it from Sydney Steel. He gets it cheaper from Germany.

So where do you stand? And the union can complain all it likes. We've complained—I was in union here. In fact, I helped organize this union in 1936. But what happens: they don't listen to people that work. Governments don't listen to the working men. Never did. The only way the working man can do is revolt. As one fellow said here—he put a paper out here. He said, "We have nothing to lose but our chains." [That was M. A. MacKenzie in the *Steelworker & Miner*, quoting Karl Marx.] That's all we have to lose, if we revolt.

And I hate to talk revolution. But I'm sure, today, if we loaded buses with about 5000 people from the city of Sydney and landed in Halifax in front of that Provincial Building in Halifax, we'd get any damn thing we wanted. If we showed enough force. But the sad part of the Sydney steelworker—Fr. Tom Boyle told me this a long time ago. He sat on one of our first conciliation boards. He was a terrific labour man. And he told me, "Frank, we're too complacent." He said, "When our stomachs are full, our brains are dead. And when our stomach gets empty, our brain goes to work. Too late. We should be thinking of our future on a full stomach, not on

5

an empty one." And it was the greatest piece of philosophy that I ever—this man, he was so right. When your stomach is full, go after it. When things are blooming, not when they're going down. It's too late to fight when they're shutting it down.

You know, there's been over a billion and a half dollars spent here in 20 years? A billion and a half! Everybody in our island could be on a pension. With the money that we wasted down there.

It's a sad picture.

(*It is a sad picture. Tell me, where does it begin for your family?*) Well, my father was the first. My father went there probably in 1913 or '14, before World War One. John Murphy. Originally they came from Ireland, but they came from Newfoundland. Came to Sydney. And he worked on the Steel Plant up until—I just forget the year he retired—1952, probably—'51 or '52. He worked in the Open Hearth.

(*Did your father want you to go on the Steel Plant?*) Oh, yeah. Well, he got me a job in the Open Hearth. See, that's where he was. My brother Pat went first—Pat went down—he was the oldest. He went to the Open Hearth. He worked at the stripper, where they take those ingots that you saw poured yesterday, and take that casing off of them. He worked up there. And my brother Tom worked up there. And my brother Sam worked up there. Three of them.

But I went on the furnaces. I liked the furnace. So I went on the furnaces in 1953. I was 20—just turned 20.

(*When you say you went on the furnaces—surely they don't just give you control over a furnace.*) Oh no, no, no. You go on as a Third Helper. Then you work your way up, from third helping to second helping to first help. On your way up, you learn the operation.

(*As a Third Helper, what did you do?*) Well, you had to carry all the stock for the furnace. Make your tapping bars to punch the hole out. There was no such thing as oxygen then to burn out a tap hole, or bombs—you had to punch them out with a big steel bar. You'd have two big billets bolted together, with a clamp. And there's a big pit, and you stood on the edge of it. Sometimes fellows fell in the pit. You know, they'd slip on the edge of the bank and fall in. We'd probably get them out before the steel came. But if they didn't, they were gone. (*Did that happen?*) Oh, yes, we had fellows killed in the Open Hearth—tap holes breaking out while they'd be working down below. The furnace would be working, the heat. The tap hole'd break out, and there would be men burned, that they would die from the effects of it, you know.

Mike Melski, shoveling at Open Hearth

I lost my leg in the Number 4 furnace there. (*How did that happen?*) Well, what happened was—we brought up our manganese—it was late getting up. I guess it was around 4 o'clock in the morning. And we wanted to get a pan off to take to another furnace. I was first helping then, on Number 4 furnace. So when the crane operator, when he lowered down the hooks—there's holes at the end of the pan—you had to reach in to get them. So Joe Cormier, my buddy, he was on the inside by the furnace. But when I reached in to get the chain, I put my foot on the track to reach the chain to push on in to him, you see—the two of them are together. He was in the heat. And I pushed the chain in. But they were charging the next furnace, and the fellow just hit the charge, and the wheel went right over and cut my foot off.

The wheel of the car. And it was loaded with manganese—one of the heaviest materials you have. So it just cut the foot right off, right at the instep.

(*When there's an accident like that in the Open Hearth, what happens? Everything stop, or what?*) Oh, no. They just take you away, keep going. There's no stopping them. They just take you—pick you up—they put you in a stretcher and take you to the hospital. But the job keeps going. There's no such thing as stopping.

They had to get a stretcher. They had to stop charging the furnace until they took me away. But that was only, probably, ten minutes. (*Where did they take you?*) Up to the emergency hospital. That little building that you saw when we were going down—that little white building. And in those days, you couldn't have your family doctor. You had to take the company doctor. When you were injured on the Steel Plant, you couldn't go to St. Rita's Hospital or the City Hospital—you had to go to the steel company hospital. They had their own doctors. This was the sad part of it, too.

(*Why is that?*) Well, they weren't competent. See, under compensation, we have a meat chart. And the less that's taken off, the less compensation you'll get. You were paid for what you lost. If they had taken me off below the knee, they'd have to pay me more—I'd have more of a disability. I'm only listed at 40 per cent. (*Because you only lost your foot.*) Only lost my foot. They give you 40 per cent disability. (*And it was the doctor at the Steel Plant that made that decision.*) Oh, yeah, they made that decision, yeah....

And 19 months after I lost the foot, I went to Halifax and had my leg taken off below the knee, so I could walk. I couldn't walk on what I had.

I don't want to tell you horror stories of compensation, but I could write a book on compensation. It's a horror story. They did skin grafts on me that were unheard of. They did five skin grafts on my carcass, where they could have taken the leg off the night I had the accident, and then it would have been all over.

When I [finally] went to Halifax and saw Dr. Allen Currie, the first question he said to me, "Frank, what butcher operated on you?" And he took my leg off in Halifax in October 1954, and I was back on the Open Hearth furnaces in May of 1955. Seven months and 20 days after he took the leg off, I was back on my own job. And I [had] spent 19 months going back and forth to this emergency hospital for those foolish operations. They even flew doctors in from Montreal to do the job. (*That's the steel company.*) The steel company. Just that meat chart.

So there's horror stories of compensation.

I went through $2^1/_2$ years off work, with a wife and five kids. I had just bought a house, just got into my home. I got in the hole about $6000. Thanks to a good grocery man that carried me. Com-

Frank Murphy: The Steel Plant Was Family

800,000 TONS OF STEEL, DECEMBER 16, 1964, HEAT #4034
Left to right: Frank Murphy, Stogick, Donald MacDonald, Ned Carew,
Don Hanrahan, Alvin MacDonald, John Neilie Campbell

pensation then was $37 a week. So you can figure where $37 would go. Paying a mortgage and feeding a family.

And when I went back to work, I had to go down to the credit union where I have some good friends, and I borrowed $6000 to pay off my bills. The first thing I did, paid off all my bills. Then it took me about eight years to pay off the $6000. This is all compensation. (*Do you mean, the results of the way compensation works?*) That's the way it works.

Let's get into the steel! (*Tell me about your work.*) I started in the Open Hearth in 1935 as a Third Helper on Number 3 furnace with Danny Yakimchuk. Now you may see a name in the paper now, Danny Yakimchuk, head of the pensioners' union. Well, that's that fellow's father that I worked with. Danny Yakimchuk. He was a First Helper. He was a Melter. They were called Melters, then. They weren't called Helpers. When you ran your furnace, they considered you a Melter. You were in charge of your furnace. You made the heat. The foreman came down and tapped it out, and put your

9

name on the sheet, and his name on the sheet. And the time—everything went on the sheet of paper. And those records are still there, right back to 1901. I don't know if they kept them all or not, but they had—a few years ago, they could tell you what heat you made.

Now, if we got a bad heat—and five years afterwards, something turned up—they could go back and say: "Frank Murphy made this heat on February 5, 1955." They could tell you what you put in it. (*In other words, if a rail failed in New York City....*) We made rails for New York Central. We made them for San Francisco Railroad, British Columbia, North Shore Quebec, CNR, CPR. And overseas, we made them for Poland, India, Pakistan. We made them for Malaysia. We made rails for everybody.

(*But I'm saying, if a rail failed in Malaysia, they could trace it back....*) Right back to the heat number. Because every rail that went out of here had the heat number on it. (*And to the person who....*) Man that made the steel that made that rail. (*That's an interesting sense of responsibility.*) Yeah, they could pinpoint you right to the minute you tapped it.

Learning on the job was something that, when the First Helper—if he liked you—he would sit down and tell you the actions to watch for in a furnace. Like, a bottom boil, on the bottom of your furnace, it would be a roll. She'd roll. But if it was an ore boil, she'd be shooting up. The sparks would be coming through the steel. And if it was a stone boil, you'd see it getting thick on the top. You'd have to put fluorspar in to cut it up. The stone'd be making it thick—like putting dumplings in a stew. That's the expression I've used: like dumplings. Well, then you'd know your stone was up. And then, if you got a bottom boil, she's boiling on the bottom, she'd roll and roll. Well, the only way we could kill a bottom boil would be put manganese in to try to stop it from rolling on the bottom.

You'd watch for even the flame in the furnace—you had your blue glasses on. You could tell [by] the flame if your furnace was hot, or cherry red, or cold, or.... (*Never cold.*) Well, what we called cold here, when she was chilling off—2500, she was chilling off. You'd want 2800 or 2900 degrees to tap out on her—rail steel.

(*So you said, sometimes, if the First Helper liked you....*) He'd tell you all this. But if he didn't like you, he wouldn't tell you anything. (*So how would you learn then?*) Well, then you'd have to probably go to another furnace or something.

See, our big trouble in our day, the men weren't educated like today. We had men operating a furnace that couldn't sign his sheet. He could make steel with anybody. They could tell you what they were doing, but they couldn't put it in writing. They'd tell you. And this is where you gained your experience.

Now, when they broke a test—they'd break it, they'd look at it. Then they could tell you what was in it. But then they would show you the different way the grain of the steel was. Or, if it got rusty right away—soon as you broke out, that it got kind of dark, and kind of like a rusted form right off the bat. They knew then they had phosphorus or sulfur; the heat was dirty. By looking at that piece of steel.

You see, it was fantastic, those men, they were steelmakers.

That's why I say we had the best steelmakers in the world here. But mind you, some of those men, now, before they learned it, we had fellows up here from the United States, from Pittsburgh, when they built the Steel Plant. And they were the first helpers we ever had here, were Americans. They brought the knowledge with them and they passed it on to everybody else.

(*And it was a matter of passing it on. In other words, am I correct that there weren't classes?*) No classes. You learned it— you either learned it, or you didn't learn it. No books. No nothing. Watching it. That's the way you learned.

I was in the fortunate position of getting with a First Helper that was very, very good—Sid MacGillivray. God have mercy on him—he's dead now. And I had the job of floating with him. That would be taking a shift off of every furnace. You know, we went to the six-day week. We were working seven days a week. But then we went to the six-day week. I went with Sid MacGillivray, float-ing. And I worked on every furnace in the Open Hearth. And I knew every heat—he was a wonderful teacher. And he would say, "Now, Frank, this is what's happening here. And this is what...."

So, when it came my turn to take a steady furnace, they wouldn't give me a steady furnace. They wanted me to stay floating. And the reason why—I knew all the furnaces. I could go to Number 3 furnace and look at it, and turn the gas or turn the oil or whatever the hell was on it, and adjust it to suit the situation. Where if they had a new man on there, he couldn't do this.

Every furnace was different, worked differently. Every one of them. You couldn't take Number 1 furnace and adjust it, and go down to Number 6 and do the same thing at Number 6. (*Even though they were all built the same.*) Yeah, all built the same. But they all had their little kinks or queeks, whatever you want to call it—they all had their little things—what you had to learn, how to get your temperature up. It was an education in itself, steelmaking.

He was a little bit on a pedestal, the First Helper. He was king-pin. "You do what I say." See. That was some of them, not all of them. Some of them were very, very good. They would take you and explain the thing to you. But some of them would try to hide it on you. Oh, yeah, they didn't want—they always figured—you see, the days before the union, if you learned [their] job, maybe they'd say, "Well, you're after my job." Especially in the foreign element, you know. Like the fellows that came from the Ukraine and those places, they always figured, "Well, my English broke, I can't talk a good English. You get my job—I go back helping." This is the theme.... But as a rule, a lot of them were very, very good. I can say that. But there were some, a few that—"You look for my job."

(*Did the workers on the Open Hearth all get together outside of work?*) Oh, yes, we'd have our banquets and everything else. We'd have a bowling banquet. Or even the shifts would get to-gether for a party, for a lobster party. Just the shift itself. See, we had—when I started, we had the A, B, and C turns—three turns, three shifts. And each shift, like, when they got on dayshift, in the evening they'd get together and go bowling. Or they'd go for a lobster do, or a fish fry, or something like that, you see.

The men were very, very close. The men in the Open Hearth. Open Hearth men were noted for being close.

For instance, if I was in Number 1 furnace and my furnace got in trouble—she was boiling on the bottom or something, or boiling on the back wall—those men are all right down with their shovels and help you. Every one of them. But that's gone today. If I was in trouble today on Number 3—that fellow on Number 2 would be sitting on his ass. You know? The attitude—the camaraderie—is all gone out of it today.

For instance, if one of our fellows died, everybody'd go to their wake. We'd go in a body. If he was sick, we'd all go in a body to hospital to see him. It was a close-knit shop. Because everybody that was on it, it was someone that you

OPEN HEARTH BOWLING LEAGUE
Seated, from left: Sam Murphy, Pat Murphy (Frank's brothers), Tony Melski, Harry Carew, Tom Smith; two young fellows are unknown. Standing: Frank Murphy, Garrett Murphy, Jimmy MacInnis, Walter Wojack.

knew personally. Now, when you became boss—I couldn't send you home, because you're so-and-so's son. So I'd hide you away and cover up for you. You know? I couldn't—geez—how? Christ, I worked with [his father]—how am I going to send this boy home? So you take him and you give him a lecturing, you know. (*Even if you had a good reason to send him home.*) Even if I had a good reason to send him home. I'd hide him, probably lock him up in one of the shacks until he's sobered up or something, if he was drunk. And then we'd do his work. We'd carry him for the shift. He'd still get his pay. This shows you, this was the camaraderie of the thing.

It was a real close shop. They were very, very close. Everybody was close.

(*It seemed to me, as I watched certain things at the plant, that there are times when you are waiting and can sit together.*) Oh, yeah. Sit together and talk. For instance, when you put your metal in a furnace—when you charge a furnace up—you put your limestone on the bottom, then you put your ore in, then you put your scrap in. Well, you've got an hour, generally, with getting your scrap soft enough, melted down enough, to put your metal in. Well, you had an hour.

Once you got your furnace cleaned up. That was the first thing, when you charge a furnace, was clean the floor. Clean the track. Then you sit down for about an hour. Well, then you talked about fishing, or going shopping, or whatever you were doing. We had a lot of fellows who were very close-knit for fishing buddies, you know.

(*In that hour....*) They'd be telling stories about the Old Country, about Newfoundland, fishing off the Grand Banks. And they'd be telling you about when they were kids in the Ukraine, they'd be telling you stories. And fellows that came from Italy, you'd hear stories from Italy. And we had all the ethnic groups that worked on the Steel Plant, all in this ward. The ethnics—that would be the Chinese and the blacks and the Ukrainians and the Swedes and the Newfoundlanders. Before 1949, Newfoundland was a foreign country. Then we had a Polish Village down over Ferris Street hill, right by the Steel Plant. Was practically all Polanders.

(*When you were in the Open Hearth, were there many black people working in the Open Hearth?*) No, no. The blacks were on the gas producer. That's where they made the gas for the Open Hearth furnace.

The first black that ever worked on an Open Hearth furnace, I had him—he came with me. During the war, I was short a man on the electric furnace, and I went in the shack, the labour shack. And I wanted one man. There was a black fellow sitting down there. And I said [to the foreman], "I'm short a man," I said, "on the electric furnace. And I want a man." He said, "Frank, there's no more men in the yard. General Yard," he said, "got all the men out. Can't get a man for you." I said, "What's wrong with him?" He looked at me like I had horns. I said, "Come on, boy, come on with me." And that was the first black that ever worked on the Open Hearth furnace—Jerome Gibson. After that, we had blacks. I said, "Boy, he got two arms and two legs and he can shovel—that's all I want. I don't care what his colour is." I never did.

(*So when we say there were all kind of ethnic groups in the....*)

14

Yeah, but the blacks were barred.... For some reason or other, the blacks—I don't know how it started or where it started—but I know there were no blacks on the Open Hearth furnace. Never saw one on it till I took that Jerome Gibson.

(*Were most of the people the same religion in the Open Hearth?*) No, no, we had every religion. But it was predominantly Catholic. Although we had quite a few other fellows, the majority of them—in those days, the Open Hearth was known as the "Vatican City." Because Peter MacIsaac was superintendent. And in the Blooming Mill it was known as the "Orange Lodge" because Bob Moffatt—he was an Orangeman or something—he ran the Blooming Mill. And then, in the Rod and Bar Mill, MacKay ran that in my time, and that was "the Masons." The Masons worked there. It was pretty well broke down. Although there were some Catholics and Protestants in all departments, predominately your religion decided where you got your job. Yeah, that went on here. Yeah, religion played a part in it....

Now, for instance, on the backshift. Now, it'd be nothing to have a big feed of herring and potatoes. We'd bring out the potatoes and the herring, have a big bucket.... Between the furnaces, we'd just pour the hot metal on the ground, and put the bucket on it and boil it, and have a big feed—or corned beef and cabbage. And a bottle of rum'd be in the cupboard, and you'd have a drink of rum

Workers in the Open Hearth Dept., 1942, including Superintendent, First, Second and Third Helpers, and charging car operator. Front, left to right: M. R. Campbell, Steve Dakai, Harold "Buster" Dawe, Jack MacAulay, _____ Drover, Angus MacDonald. Back: Frank MacArthur, Ed Hartigan, Dick Rogers, Tom Peddle, Charlie MacDonald, John MacDonald, Ned Walsh, Joe MacLean, John Tobin, Leo O'Leary.

or something. The old-timers are more so for the rum, you know. You'd take your furnace shovel and you'd just wash it off, and then you'd put the capelin on it, and put it in front of a peephole. In the furnace, where you take the test out. And you'd fry your capelin there, right on the shovel.

(*Have a meal together.*) Oh, yeah. The furnace crew would do that. Whatever crew—like, if I was on Number 3, we'd have herring and potatoes, probably, and next night we'd have corned beef and cabbage. But you still bring your lunch out. Because we worked the long hours. We were working 11 by day and 13 by night. We'd go to 7 o'clock in the morning and come home, and then the other shift would come out at 5 o'clock and stay till the next morning. And on Sunday, if you were changing—going from backshift to dayshift—you went out on Sunday morning at 7, and you came home Monday morning. Twenty-four hours, you never came home at all.

I was there for—I was nine days short of 45 years.

(*When you and I went in the Open Hearth yesterday, there was just one furnace in operation.*) When I was there, there were 12. (*And you could look the length of that and there'd be all these men working....*) At their furnace. Every one. Different times, they'd be tapping out. Each fellow would be doing something different in that time. And you knew every one of them, and you knew what they were [doing]— you knew what their family [was up to]—they'd come and tell you their family troubles and everything else, you know.

That was one of our big downfalls here, you know, was this being a family plant. It didn't make any difference whether you could do your job, if you were a son of so-and-so. (*Is that right?*) Oh, yeah, you got a job. If you didn't fit in on that job, they put you somewhere else. But if you were in Hamilton or Algoma, they'd fire you. But here, they just moved you somewhere else.

Well, you see, we were born with the Steel Plant in our back door. Look out in the morning and you'd see the smoke come out of the stacks. And you'd go to school—school was right up here; the convent was right up here—the Steel Plant. Every kid going to school knowing when the Blast Furnace was dumping or charging. Then at nighttime when they used to dump the slag in the water, the sky'd all light up, everyone would know. So everybody knew what the Steel Plant was.

There were 27 men worked with me in the Open Hearth—we were all born in the same year. All 1914 babies....

Went to wakes and weddings and everything, together. We went in a group. We'd leave the plant at 11 o'clock in the night and go to a fellow's house. The wakes were all in the houses then, you know. If one of our men died, everybody went in and knelt down and said the rosary, no matter if he was Catholic, Protestant, or what he was. Everybody knelt down and said their prayers. That was common. Common thing. And they'd all go to the funeral. If he was on our shift, that died, we'd all change the whole shift to go to the funeral.

(*And what about paying for the funeral?*) Well, we always took a collection up. And anyone who was off sick, the men took up a collection. You could get anything from $2000 down to $50. It would depend on the man himself, mostly. You know, if you were well liked.

And anyone that was joining the priesthood or becoming a minister or anything, they took up a collection for him, to send him away. Say, for instance, if I had a son who wanted to study for the ministry. Well, they'd take up a collection and give him maybe $100 or $150. The men would all chip in. (*The men on the Open Hearth.*) Yes.

(*I bet if someone was getting married....*) They'd do the same thing. Everybody got a wedding present from the shift. No matter who died, there was always a mass card if he was a Catholic, got flowers if he was a Protestant. That was organized. We had our own little mutual benefit, in our own time. We paid 25 cents a week into it. And if you were off sick, you got $10 every week for 13 weeks, from our department. But that was our own self-organization. We did that on our own. (*It wasn't the union.*) Oh, no, no, no, just the men themselves. In fact, I was president of ours.

If you worked in the Open Hearth and you were building a house—we had 35 or 40 men up there that worked on the backshift. And there was no such thing as a cement mixer. We'd have four big boards going, and mix it all by hand, and build a foundation. Maybe it took you 10 hours to build it. And then you went back to work that night. You put in the whole foundation before you left, by hand.... Come and help you build it and everything.

It was family. The Steel Plant was family. All family. And it didn't make a difference if you were black, white, or what it was, if you were building a house. We had an old coloured fellow down there—he was putting a foundation under it. So we'd go down there and we'd dig it out, and we'd put in his cribwork for him and all his forms—bunch of men. And our electricians went down and did the wiring—fellows that were electricians on the Steel Plant—they went down and did the wiring. Everybody helped everybody.

But the sad part of the whole thing was—and I hate to say this—when we became unionized, there was something about it that dropped off. Because you were guaranteed five days or six days a week.

Now, when I went in there, for instance, if the mill was going down half time, we didn't lay anybody off like they do today. We would split the shifts. A married man worked four, and a single man would take three. And nobody was laid off. We all got a share. But once the union came in and demanded you get six days a week, well, that went out the window. That was sometime in the '40s, during the war.

But in the early years of my time, from '34 to '40, we wired houses for fellows. We even took a bunch of electricians out, when they built St. Augustine's Church out there on Grand Lake Road, and wired it for the priests down there. It was all steel company.

(*And would people also make things on the plant that could be used in their homes?*)

Well, it was all coal stoves then. They'd make pokers, and they'd make grates for their stoves. The Foundry had all the patterns for practically every stove. If I wanted a grate, I'd go up and I'd see the foreman in the Foundry. And on the backshift they'd make a grate for you or they'd make a damper for you. If you'd want something done, they'd do it. And if you knew him, or if you were a good friend of him up there, he'd pour you a brass hot-water front for your stove—one that would last a lifetime. And if I ask him for five of them in five days— I got five brass hot-water fronts.

And if you wanted a poker made, or a set of tongs to take the

18

clinkers out of your furnace, you'd go out there. And the next thing you know, they're laying there. No one sees it, but they're laying there. You don't know who put it there, but you know where it came from. No one would come down and present it to you.

For instance, like when a foundry car would be coming down, he would call me and say, "Now, look at Number 2 box there." So I'd go over to Number 2 box and scrape the sand away, and the hot-water front would be buried on the car. Well, he never gave it to me. I found it on the car. I don't know who made it. I never saw it being made. But it was there.

(*How would you get things like that out of the plant?*) Oh, it took a little bit of conniving to get it out.

If you had a friend that had a car in there. And if you were— like, the superintendent—if I went to the superintendent and said, "Look, I got an iron front made," he'd give me a pass to take it out as scrap. You'd carry it out.

At that time you could go up and buy scrap. Well, say you got

Inside the Machine Shop

10 pounds—oh, 50 cents or a dollar, at the General Office, and he'd give you a slip to take it out. Same way with nails. If you were building a house and you wanted nails, you'd get an order for 50 pounds of nails. So you'd go in on the plant, and you'd come out with maybe two kegs of nails. When you'd pass the fellow at the gate, he got the slip. He doesn't check—they never checked you out in those days. (*So it went out as scrap.*) You bought a piece of scrap.

Actually, it was brand-new nails.

I remember one time one of our watchmen caught a fellow with a lunch can full of nails. He was over before the chief, and the chief gave the watchman hell for saying a word. He said, "Why don't you catch some of those fellows that are going with 10 kegs of nails?" he said. "Never mind the fellow with the lunch can." Gave him hell for catching the fellow—that's the way it was.

Everybody knew everybody. If I had a friend of mine that got into trouble, I could go up and talk to the chief. I knew him. I'd say, "Look," I said, "Chief, he's got five kids. And he's just getting along, and he's having...." "Oh, send him back to work."

I don't know what it was, but there was something that—I had a camaraderie with all of them, that I could talk to most any of them. From Clem Anson [a general manager; see Chapter 9]—one fellow asked me, he said one time, "How can you talk to Clem Anson like that?" I said, "Clem Anson's only a man." As I said before, he's no better than I. He's got a better job, and I call him Mr. Anson. But there's no reason why I can't talk to him. He's not God. No, he was just another human being.

And that's been my philosophy all my lifetime.

(*But you do make it clear there was the sense of family, the sense of caring for one another in the Open Hearth—or in the Steel Plant in general perhaps.*) Generally—the whole thing. Like, the Blast Furnace had the same thing—they had their own benefit society, that they paid people $10 a week. And $10 a week then was a lot of money.

Now I can tell you this. I remember being laying in my bed home, after my leg was off. And two men came in the bedroom. And they threw a bunch of money on the bed—couple of bagfuls. There was anything from a one to a twenty, and silver. And I counted

20

DISCO Machine Shop, 1950. Back row, left to right: Harry Tobin, Ron Adams, Ernie Yates, Rice Gaudet, Jim MacKillop, Albert Hennick, Gerard MacNeil, Ed Hubley, L.J. (Lem) Evans. Front: Monty Mortimer, Alfred Evans, Berkly Evans, Howard Macdonald, Bill Fedora

$2000, that they collected at the Steel Plant for me when I was off. They made it plant-wide—they got at the paymaster—made it plant-wide. I got over $2000. And they did that on two different occasions while I was off work.

So when you're dealing with those kind of people, those people are human. They're human beings. You're not just a statistic or a number with them. Those are people that—you associate your life with, and you're working with them. And if they don't feel good, now.... For instance, if a fellow came out and he said, "Geez, I've got an awful cold." "Now, you go in the shack and stay there for the night. And we'll open the hole and we'll mud the runner."

You looked after them.

(*And you're telling me the truth here? You're not trying to make the Open Hearth, or the workers, look better than they were, are you?*) Oh, no.

This is the way they worked. It was one big family. (*Ah, but there must have been some rotten people like in any family.*) Oh, yes. We had a few of them, too. That's why I say, I don't want to name any of them. But we had fellows, too, were just as miserable. We had fellows who wouldn't turn their hand to help you. But mind you, they'd pay for it in the long run. Once you knew them.

I remember going to a man one time, taking up a collection. And we were only asking 50 cents—that was a lot of money, then. And he said, "No, I save my money. I'm not going to give you any money." Okay. But that man got sick one time. And who did he call, looking for somebody to take a collection? He called me. And I said, "Boy, you remember when I asked you for 50 cents? Now," I said, "tough.... You go and get somebody else to take up a collection for you."

And you knew everybody. You knew the fellows who were carrying stories to the bosses. You'd set traps for them, you know. I can tell you of one incident. We had one fellow, boy. We were wondering how the stories were getting out. We couldn't fathom it at all. But we had an idea. So anyway, this fellow came into the shack one day and he sat down. And I started running down one of the superintendents. He had just come on, boy, and I was calling him—he was from England. And I called him everything under the sun. And about an hour afterwards, this man walked in the shack. And he came right to me. "Oh, Frank," he said, "you think I'm quite a prick, don't you?" And I started to laugh. "Well," I said, "thanks, Jack," I said. "I didn't mean a word I said. I think you're a wonderful guy. And so do all the fellows here. But," I said, "we had a fellow carrying stories. Now I know who he is."

(*And then what do you do with a fellow like that?*) Well, then you ignore him. He has no life after that at all. You just ignore him. Walk by him like he was a stick. Naturally, after maybe two or three months you'll find he either shifted to another place, on the back of the mill somewhere. But he doesn't stay on the furnace with you. You ignore him that bad—you make life so miserable for him that he doesn't stay there.

[From Frank's notebook:] "July 24, 1971. Number 1 furnace, first test, 11 carbon, 100 sulfur. That was 4:06. We tapped her at 7:30,

on 65 sulfur and 3 carbon. We put 15 bags of coke in the ladle. Heat boiled in ladle, added 10 boxes of manganese extra, and 6 more bags of coke. Heat finished, 58 sulfur, 23 carbon, for tie plate."

But the story behind that was: when I went out there at 4 o'clock in the afternoon, Gonzales said, "Frank, we'll take her for scrap." Rather than make [steel]—the sulfur was 100 sulfur. I said, "No, we'll make something. We'll make tie plate." Because I knew they'd [allow] over 60 sulfur on tie plate. He said, "You've got no carbon." I said, "That's all right." So I put the oxygen right down on the bath. And I got her stinking hot. And I kept adding stone, and taking slag off.

So anyway, we threw everything in the ladle. And I got all the helpers out of the way. I said, "Okay, take her over, boy." Took her over, and the flames went right up clean to the roof of the Open Hearth. We had no carbon; we had to add coke. But the heat finished 23 carbon and 58 sulfur for tie plate. We made something [of it].... We made a product that you could sell.

So, you keep at it. Like a bulldog, you stay in there, you stay with it, until you get something.

We were steelmakers. The period of steelmaking has gone to computer. Everything that goes into this [new electric arc] furnace, what I gather—everything is computer. They just push the buttons and they make everything—all the additions are done.

Well, in my day, boy, you had to wrack your brain, boy, to know what was going on. When that heat went in the ladle, you were a human calculator. Everything was by the clock. I'd look—my manganese is going to be in five minutes, and then it's going to start to disintegrate. I'm going to lose it. So I've got $4^1/_2$ minutes to get the manganese in. I've got to get a tap hole open, and I've got to get the silicon into the ladle. And nobody talks to you—even the superintendent don't bother you then. The wheels are—everything is going full blast, knowing your calculations and what you're going to do.

And then you get a furnace that breaks out on you. And you've got 100 carbon, and she's going out in the ladle. And you want to keep the oxygen on to get her down to 75. And you know you're losing X-number of points per minute. And you're saying, "I've got three minutes—I've got 90 carbon—I've got 80 carbon—I've got 75 carbon. Turn her over!" You know your timing—you know, you get so many points per minute....

When you see the flame go right up through and set fire to those cranes, that you had to get up with a fire extinguisher to put the grease out. The crane'd be burning—the grease'd be burning up on the top of those girders. And they'd still be pouring the heat, and there'd be men up with fire extinguishers putting it out. Walking out on those girders over that hot ladle.

You know, sometimes, in order to catch a heat. Say a carbon is down, we'll say, to 40, and you're making 70-carbon rails. That means that you have to put 30 bags of coke in that ladle, and every one of them weigh over 60 pounds. And you had to throw it in. And you have a bunch of men lined up, and they just put their coats over their heads and they just throw one at a time, and keep going around in a circle, trying to get the coke in for you before she'd foam out of the ladle, you know....

And all those little technical things that they don't print. They don't put this in books, you see.

You know, I could talk steel all day, I could talk steel for a month. That's all I do! *Frank laughs.* Ask me anything else, I wouldn't know!

CHAPTER 2

The Steel Boom
Comes to Sydney, 1899

"By and by, when Pittsburgh is a village and New York has got
to be whistled for to stop a steamboat, Sydney will be the grand
seaport of a continent."—*Sydney Daily Record*, 1901.

Sydney is a boom town. It has a boom town shape, with industry
established right through the heart of it. It still reflects the vulner-
ability and volatility of a one-industry town: an ethnic composition
rooted in those first years, a conservative mercantile class, a history of outside control, and a focus outside the community for future development, with consequent paternalism and dependency—

and PROMISE. Throughout the Steel Boom (1899-1901), there is a religious tone in speeches and newspaper reports. It can be argued that any huge change can provoke a response couched in older forms of expression—when participants have not lived with that change long enough to find the appropriate words to describe it. And often in the period of the Steel Boom, a religious ambiance is evoked.

In this chapter we look at some of the events around the establishment of the iron and steel plant in Sydney, hoping to evoke some of the experience, the tone and timbre of those events. While there is a beginning and an end, no attempt is made to narrate all events, or even to keep them in order. Instead, we present a variety of perspectives on the Steel Boom from 1899 to 1902, the "era of unlimited optimism," from the incorporation of Dominion Iron and Steel and the start of construction, to the making of the first steel and industrialist Henry Whitney's departure.

Henry M. Whitney—the American promoter who in 1893 consolidated the Cape Breton mines into the Dominion Coal Company—may have considered a steel plant here as early as 1897, when experiments at the Ferrona Works of the mainland Nova Scotia Steel Company proved that Dominion's coal could be used for steelmaking. He proposed a merger with Scotia Steel in New Glasgow, was turned down, and began seeking "encouragement" to establish a steel works in Cape Breton.

Whitney found encouragement at all three levels of government: in federal bounties, in provincial relief on coal royalties, in free land and free water and tax relief from the ratepayers of Sydney. The prospectus the company issued in 1901 included as one of the stock's selling points the fact that it expected to receive over eight million dollars in bounties on iron and steel production. The opposition in the House of Commons, fearing that the demands on the government would be unduly large, wondered if the bounties could not be limited, arguing that this was not a struggling industry: "with twenty-eight million dollars capital and the support of great financial magnates, it could hardly be contended that the bounty was essential to success." The federal Minister of Finance, W. S. Fielding—the man who had done so much at the *provincial*

26

level to help Whitney create Dominion Coal Company in 1893—countered that a large cost to the country was the risk taken when the bounties were offered.

Whitney approached the provincial government to see what they would put up to get a steel plant underway. His letter to Premier George Murray, presented to the Nova Scotia Legislature in February 1899, mentioned a number of benefits a steel plant would bring to the province. These promises would be repeated again and again as the steel plant was promoted: that the use of more coal would result in steady, year-round, expanded work at the mines; that Nova Scotians forced to leave to find work could now come home; and that spin-off industries, especially shipbuilding to restore Nova Scotia's former glory, would surely come in the wake of iron and steel production.

Herman Melville Whitney, president of Dominion Coal Company and Dominion Iron and Steel Company. One newspaper wrote that it was good that a new street had been named Whitney, so that "years from now, when the steel plant is only a memory, we will remember, if not the founder, at least the finder, of Sydney."

Whitney asked the government for 100 per cent relief from paying royalties on all coal used in connection with the steel plant, for five years. What he got was 50 per cent relief from royalties for eight years. The incorporated company was also empowered "to expropriate any land it required and could not obtain by private treaty." Eventually the provincial government would amend the act of incorporation to allow the company to pay dividends to stockholders *during* the construction phase. One Member of the Legislative Assembly stood to put himself on record regarding this "objectionable" clause: "He did not think he wanted to have it said abroad that the Nova Scotia Legislature would grant almost anything."

From the February 1899 *Island Reporter*:

The people of Cape Breton County are determined that everything

Dominion Iron and Steel Company workers
at the iron ore deposit at Bell Island, Newfoundland

which possibly lays in their power and within the sphere of their influence ought to be attempted to bring ahead the location of the iron industry as a fixture in our midst. The people of this county are most anxious for the settlement within our borders of this great industry and all its accompaniments of increased labour, wide business prosperity, and general commercial expansion, and it is part of wisdom to take time by the forelock in this patriotic matter....

Cape Breton is the natural hunting ground today for the corporation which desires to invest its capital with sure and large returns from iron developments. Cape Breton's advantages...have so to speak been tested in a furnace seven times heated.... We cannot therefore doubt, whether the time that elapses be long or short, that this county will become the Birminghan and Glasgow of Canada as today it is the Newcastle and Cardiff of the Dominion.... Cape Breton has no enemy except Time itself. The great iron enterprise and commercial industrial life can only be delayed in its coming, its coming can never be prevented. Let every Cape Bretonian lay that fact to heart and it must have its legitimate fruit in a more exalted faith in our position, a more devoted zeal towards united action all along the line, and the loosening of that critical and

The Steel Boom Comes to Sydney, 1899

Workers at Marble Mountain, Cape Breton, quarry limestone for the Steel Plant

pessimistic spirit which doth so easily beset us. If capital once makes up its mind to come to this county it will come, and that without undue delay, and to stay.

The extent to which the people of Sydney were willing to go to get the steel plant built in their town is indicated by a passage from Dr. A. S. Kendall's speech for re-election in October 1900:

We saved the people of the town of Sydney from themselves. In our desperately poor condition, 3 years ago, a meeting was held in Sydney in which there was not a dissenting voice, and a vote passed empowering the Legislature of Nova Scotia to exempt steel works, that might be erected in the town of Sydney, from taxation forever.... [We] ventured to ignore that mandate....

What Sydney *did* give was about 450 acres of land valued at $83,000, a free water supply, and exemption from taxation for 30 years. There was also the implicit understanding that the town would undertake whatever measures proved necessary to accommodate such an expanded populace as iron and steel would bring.

It was realized that having the steel plant in place was only the beginning. Announcing that it would definitely be established at Sydney, the *Industrial Advocate* wrote: "Its main influence will be

to promote various subsidiary industries which will naturally clus-
ter around and grow up with the larger undertaking." This was a
continuing theme. Whitney would repeat it in September in his
speech to the people of Sydney:

Industries that depend upon the production of these metals are bound
to follow. I have no doubt...and unless I am greatly mistaken, before
many years the production of this vast concern will stretch from Atlantic
to the Pacific, and the material manufactured be exhibited in all marts of
the world. To the province of Nova Scotia will be restored its old shipbuilding industry.

The August *Industrial Advocate* suggested a manufacturer of
agricultural implements be sought as soon as the iron works would
open, and said that it had been "reported" that the Montreal Rolling Mills had opened negotiations to locate in Sydney. But above
all, the hope was shipbuilding:

When then a number of hard-headed, wealthy, widely experienced,
shrewd businessmen have a vision of a vast shipbuilding industry being
established at Sydney, we take it that, in Shelley's words, there is likely
to be another illustration of the mind creating "the thing it contemplates."

But the *Industrial Advocate* recognized that it would require
more than "contemplation" to get that shipbuilding industry or any
other. There were assurances required

that iron and coal would be permanent; that no fiscal or political
changes are likely to bring danger to the enterprise; that the foundations
of cheap material and labour will not be disturbed; and that industry will
have a clear course unobstructed by anything except fair competition,
which is not feared.... The high character and business ability of the men
engaged...leave little doubt that the project will assume vast proportions
and that there is opening up for Cape Breton an era of prosperity in
which the whole province will share.

By August of 1902 the *Industrial Advocate* wrote:

[The *Island Reporter*] pleads for further measure of manufacturing
enterprise in connection with the steel industry at Sydney.... An English
manufacturer...intimates...he will establish a plant for manufacture of
finished products in iron wherever the best inducements are offered.... If
it is a question of a bonus [continued the *Industrial Advocate*], we see no
reason why something in this direction could not be done. We bonused

Sydney's Mayor Crowe

the steel works, and we are likely to offer a bonus to shipbuilding, and why should an industry such as we are considering not be encouraged. It is admitted by all that industries of this nature are badly needed in Sydney at the present juncture.

These spin-off industries did not come.

But Henry Melville Whitney *did* come to Sydney. Under the headline "SOURCE OF ALL PROSPERITY" the August 1899 newspaper described "Sydney's Great Public Demonstration in Honour of Henry M. Whitney, President of the Dominion Iron and Steel Company":

Long before the strains of the band had ceased the ancient hall was crammed to the very buttresses, and beyond and above rolled a perfect sea of expectant faces. Mingled with the subdued voices that sounded like the murmur of a quiet surge upon a rock-bound shore, one could imagine the echoes of tones long since passed away—the eloquence of days of yore. Gone, gone, with the dust, for are we not beginning a new life? But the calm of the assembly was soon destined to break into a tempest. At the appearance of Mr. Whitney...a shout like the shout of a storm arose, and white handkerchiefs waved in the air like curling foam on the crest of the waves.

Truly, it was a brilliant function, and the personification of all that was best and noblest in the town. The church, the law, medicine, commerce, art, mining, agriculture, and army and navy, were all splendidly represented....

Behind Mr. Whitney and the mayor, at the rear of the platform, arose the legend: "Sydney Welcomes Henry M. Whitney," beneath which was ingeniously draped the American and Canadian ensigns, a design that was repeated upon a more modest scale upon every wall. On the southern wall, a motto in brilliant lettering read, "Iron Development is the Gauge of National Prosperity," and on the northern, "Canada Should by all Means Encourage Iron Production." Knots of evergreens were disposed tastefully about, and tiers of flowers depended from the galleries and the edge of the platform and the gallery itself looked like a fairy garden.

Views from the Steel Plant

[Mayor Crowe offered a speech of welcome to Whitney, including:]

"Long before the mineral resources of Cape Breton attracted your attention as affording an inviting and promising field for large investments, your fame had been wafted to our shores, and we knew somewhat of you as a successful financier and promoter of great enterprises, as a man of sound judgment, vast energy and broad views....

"It is not too much to expect that, as the outcome of it, this part of Canada, by reason of its mineral wealth, commanding position and other advantages, will within a few years become the seat of extensive manufacturing industries, and that the whole of the Dominion of Canada will profit largely by the operations recently commenced by your company at Sydney...."

After the applause which greeted the address had subsided, Mr. Whitney rose to respond, but his appearance was so rapturously received that he was forced to remain some time standing before he could attempt to speak. He said:

"I am here not only as a private citizen, but I find myself in a public capacity with certain public duties to perform....

"We are exceedingly pleased with the location which you have so liberally provided for us. I desire here and now to thank the mayor and council of Sydney, who have enabled us to proceed so promptly with the construction....

"I believe that the foundation of this huge industry will be ready before the close of the year, and next summer these immense buildings, which are to produce wealth and prosperity in your land, will begin to rise rapidly before your eyes. Those interested are largely citizens of Canada, and the capital itself is chiefly drawn from the Dominion, and the personnel of the directorate are your own countrymen....

"We are henceforth and forever to be partners together in this great enterprise. We could not if we would be separate. To me is allotted the task of developing in your midst this huge industry; to you belong the care of the home and the social life. My task is, perhaps, easier than yours. To neither will it be a merry march to the music of flutes and soft recorders....

"You have your water systems, your sewerage, your street regulations, your lighting, and various other duties, before you. All these facilities must be immediately procured. The question of your drainage is very material, and I would advocate the citizens of this town that they cannot too soon take up the subject of laying out streets, and that they cannot, for the sake of themselves and future generations, allow further inattention to a well regulated sewage system. Thoroughly assured sanitary conditions means security to life.

"I believe that the establishment of these iron works will be the means of introducing the town of Sydney to the length and breadth of the whole world. I cannot control my enthusiasm when I think of the future. The dormant energies of the country will be awakened. Here, right at our very doors, is the basic source of all prosperity. We know that on yonder spot all the elements that go to produce iron and steel can be assembled cheaper than on any other spot on the face of the earth. We have limestone almost at our feet, immense coal fields right at hand, and magnificent iron areas within a few hours sail from the centre of production. It has been demonstrated that Cape Breton coal is the best in the world for metallurgical purposes....

"You have expressed a wish that I shall become one of you. I have no other choice, and I am delighted to be able to meet your desires. Know that hereafter my life and my lot is one with you. To this spot, by mysterious means, have my feet been guided. 'There is a destiny that shapes our ends, rough hew them how we will.'

"The establishment of the iron and steel works signifies more than the works alone. Industries that depend upon the production of these metals are bound to follow. I have no doubt that there will be a gradual extension from one thing to another, and, unless I am greatly mistaken, before many years the production of this vast concern will stretch from the Atlantic to the Pacific, and the material manufactured be exhibited in all the marts of the world.

"To the province of Nova Scotia will be restored its old shipbuilding industry....

"To me belongs the duty of expanding commercially the influence of these works. Another and more momentous duty is yours—the expansion of the influence of the home and social morality. I can assure you that there is nothing that affords me more concern than the character of your civic administration. You must demand through your suffrages a domestic government that will ensure virtuous homes and healthful lives.

The direction of domestic conditions requires from you the utmost care and solicitude, for are not good moral laws purchased by that eternal vigilance which is the price of liberty? Enforcement of sumptuary regulations in your midst is of the first importance. Who is so strong that he can guard himself from temptation? The voice of fathers and mothers, and those to whose care is confided the protection of the home and fireside, goes up to heaven laden with the prayer, 'Lead Us Not Into Temptation.' If you have laws which regulate the traffic in strong drink let the moral strength of the community manifest

Blast Furnace under construction. The first fire was lit on February 2, 1901. The first cast of pig iron was poured on February 6.

itself in a vigorous co-operation with your civic representatives in their endeavor to have those regulations enforced.

"We are now bound together in the indissoluble ties of friendship. I will, on my part, make the name of Sydney resound far and wide. For the healthy social life and the moral prosperity of the people rest with you and not with me. It is your duty to mould the character of the youthful generation. But my efforts in this direction will always be at your disposal. In conclusion, let me express my gratitude for the sentiment that prompted you to offer me the opportunity to meet you publicly, and let me assure you that it is my earnest hope that the memory and influence of this assembly will survive to the end of time." *Loud and prolonged applause.*

After the mayor had announced that an opportunity would be given to the citizens to meet Mr. Whitney on the platform, the Sydney cornet band played with musical vigor and emphasis, the "Star-Spangled Banner."

By December 1899, 1500 men were at work on construction, and it was expected to rise to 3000 by spring.

The editor of the *Baddeck Telephone* addressed the people of Victoria County:

There are those who, in the prosperity of others, see only misery for themselves. That is not our nature. We rejoice with those that do rejoice. But there is more than philosophy in our pleasure.... Coincident with the advancement of Sydney will come our prosperity. These people must be fed. When we drive through the glens of Victoria County, when we look upon the thousands of fertile acres yearning for the plow, the verdant hillside pastures inviting great flocks of sheep to crop their verdure; the thought weighs upon us that a future is yet in store for our little island of which we hardly yet have dreamed.... The buyers will soon be at our doors; prepare now for a good harvest. Next summer, roots, table vegetables, mutton and veal should all sell.

And again in November:

The boom that has swept its tidal wave around the ancient garrison town of Sydney and buried its dead past in the foam of bustle and business, is...one of those lucky accidents, not uncommon on the American continent, where some favoured spot affords exceptional facilities for a certain line of trade or manufacture. It would be surprising indeed if all the extravagant prophesies of future greatness should be realized. There is a sea level in the commercial world that affects all great enterprises, yet between the horizon and top of the rosy dawn streak there is room.... Our farmers have at their doors what they so long have mourned for, that is a market. Remember, however, they will have competition, very strong competition, in the quality of their products.... Taking all round there is a chance for the farmer.

Cape Breton farmers were unable to rise to this challenge, certainly not in these first years. According to C. W. Vernon in *Cape Breton, Canada* [1903], the local market "is at present supplied almost entirely from outside the island." He was referring not only to fruits and vegetables, but to milk and butter as well. S. T. Woods, in the *Toronto Globe*, wrote of some good farmland in Cape Breton and beef production in Prince Edward Island, but due to dampness and insufficient sunshine for wheat growing, plus a

manifest disinclination toward farming work..., the result is a large volume of trade between the island and the leading commercial centres of Ontario. This is not international trade, although the Sydney people talk of the supplies they import "from Canada," and it is not recorded in any official tabulation. But it is nonetheless important.... The flour consumed in Sydney and throughout Cape Breton Island is largely produced in Ontario.... Manitoba flour has also a large sale. The butter trade is of considerable importance, and much is shipped directly from Toronto. Ontario supplies the island with cheese, and in addition to the trade in food supplies large quantities of manufactured goods and building materials come from the producing centres of Ontario and Quebec.

Even hay was being imported. Dead meat was coming down in refrigerated cars and Prince Edward Island, not knowing the market, was asking "fantastic prices" and could not compete. In short, the only thing rural Cape Breton seemed to have supplied to booming Sydney in any quantity was young men to serve as unskilled labourers.

C. W. Vernon reported:

The influx of population to the Sydneys and the mining districts is having the effect of reducing the annual catch at many places, owing to the fact that many fishermen have been led to seek what they believe to be more remunerative employment.

The inspector of the schools in 1903 reported:

In Victoria County, sections were vacant during the year. A number of these had few or no pupils and others have been so weakened by the removal of many families into the mining and industrial centers of the island, that they were unable to support schools.

Precisely how many native Cape Bretoners moved, and the proportions per county, is not clear. But Ronald F. Crawley, working with the 1901 census, offers some suggestions toward a portrait of the work force gathered at Sydney. The town grew from 3000 in 1891 to 9909 in 1901.

There were 6246 immigrants in Cape Breton County. "...3392 were from Newfoundland, 1553 from the British Isles, 679 from the United States, 110 from Italy, 94 from Russia, 92 from France,

82 from Norway and Sweden, 68 from Austria-Hungary, 60 from Syria, and the remainder from various other countries." Cape Breton County was the only county on the island to increase in population, and that increase was the largest of any county in Nova Scotia. It should be added that this continued to be a very mobile work force; a study of street directories revealed that for every ten people that arrived, seven left.

The bulk of the accidents at the Steel Plant seemed to happen to Newfoundlanders, which may be indicative of the kinds of work they were asked to do, and also their high proportion in the plant. The bulk of trouble reported in the papers was linked to Italians. There were 211 arrests in Sydney in the first three months of 1901. Over and over, Italians were in court, reported as fighting, stealing money and wives from one another, retaliating with guns, picks, and knives. So frequent were arrests at the Coke Ovens and the Pier that a new police station was situated in that vicinity. Trying to discuss the cosmopolitan nature of Sydney, the *Daily Record* revealed various attitudes that would crop up again in times of labour tension. Regarding the Italians specifically, it said they were "getting a bad press because of a few 'black sheep.'" It then went on to say: "The trouble with the quarrelsome Italian is that he resorts to the knife or other weapons when aroused, unlike his more northern neighbour."

When Newfoundland newspapers reported men coming back without having found work in Sydney, the *Daily Record* responded:

They must have sought work in the wrong places or they want work they are unable to do.... Newfoundlanders would doubtless be taken on in preference to Germans or Austrians or Negroes, if the latter are not skilled workmen. Some foolish protests have been heard in town with regard to the arrival of colored iron workers, but prejudice of this kind is irrational. It is a peculiarly American prejudice and very un-British. We shall doubtless soon hear a prolonged wail about the importation of Austrians. But this feeling is not against the Negroes and foreigners alone. It will be remembered that a fuss was made some months ago over the employment on the streets of some men who did not belong to Sydney. It is doubtful whether the Board of Works would venture to employ residents of Ward Three to work on the street in Ward Five.

Views from the Steel Plant

David Baker, the new general manager of DISCO [Dominion Iron and Steel Company], spoke of their hiring practices:

Neither religion nor nationality enters into the creed of the company.... But we only employ as few skilled labour as we possibly can because we have to pay them higher wages. We depend upon the home labour to get broken in.

The *Sydney Post* was less careful about foreigners:

Two cars filled with Italians arrived in town last night. The importation of so many foreigners augers ill for labour in Cape Breton next season. [About a week later:] Another batch of Italians for Sydney arrived yesterday on the steamer *Lusitania* at Halifax. Cape Breton is now about flooded with foreigners and there are more to come.

A group of Italians was sent to work at the Inverness mines. They were driven away by the natives. The *Post* published a letter signed "Judique on the Floor," considering the Scotchmen "slandered" just because "the brave boys of Inverness had the wisdom and pluck to drive from their shores the most undesirable class of people known. Organ grinders," he called them, "Mafia of the coke ovens, holy terrors."

The fear of cheap foreign labour was clear in a letter to the editor (*Post*, 1902): "One Yankee is as good as two niggers and one Canadian as good as two Yankees."

Crawley has pointed out that the newspapers did *not* turn on DISCO, whose agents searched the world for both skilled and unskilled, recruiting laid-off workers from plant closures in Germany, available ironworkers and construction men in Alabama and Pittsburgh, and the Italian labourers.

Tensions within the work force showed themselves in the first years: divisions between union and non-union, skilled and unskilled, native and foreign worker. At the same time, ideas of unionism were introduced by American workers and Glace Bay miners. Workers at the Steel Plant participated in the international fight for the nine-hour day, and at one point 400 people were off the job. But they also saw examples of scabbing, of failures due to lack of solidarity. The first major strike came in 1904, and it was lost largely because of divisions among the workers. It would be 1909 before they struck as a unified class.

Perhaps the most significant element in the labour disputes during the first years was the local media's general response, and the attitude it revealed toward the workmen generally. A strike was lost at the Coke Ovens, where men demanded $1.75 a day instead of $1.50—which "does not seem unreasonable [to the reporter], as things go in Sydney at present"—referring to the inflated cost of everything. However, the strike was "an ill-advised affair. The strikers must have known there was no chance of a mere handful of men, unsupported and with little sympathy from the community at large, succeeding against a powerful company in whose success the town and the country at large is so deeply interested."

The expressed attitudes regarding the dangers of the steel works were equally unsympathetic. The *Ottawa Citizen General* reported on 61 deaths and many injuries in the first two years of the plant. "The works have been termed a human slaughterhouse." Sydney's *Daily Record* responded: "While there is a grain of truth in the foregoing, yet no citizen of Sydney will feel but that it contains an injustice to both the town and the company. There are certain occupations in which the risk to human life is greater than average."

There were a great number of drinking establishments, especially at the Coke Ovens and the Pier—and temperance representatives were often at Town Council, demanding that the Scott Act [the Canadian Prhohibition Act] be summarily imposed. They insisted the streets of Sydney were no longer safe at night.

Rosslyn Rink had opened and a variety of shows were offered, including Gilbert and Sullivan operettas. Still it was felt Sydney needed a real theatre, not a skating rink.

"Mayor Crowe organized a series of lectures to popularize the study of sanitary science and domestic hygiene, as well as music, language, American literature and authors, world discoverers"—and these were apparently well enough attended. Mark Sullivan, writing for the *Boston Transcript* (quoted in the *Post*), indicated that it was hard to hold onto skilled American workmen: "Sydney in its present state of development is about the most hideously ugly and unattractive place in America." It was 24 hours from Boston and "a hundred miles from the knowledge of God." Sullivan continued:

Views from the Steel Plant

It is small wonder the American workman is willing to come here, induced by free fare and the prospect of novelty; it is equally small wonder he is unwilling to stay when he knows work is plenty at home. A corporation founding a new plant must balance the difficulty and cost of collecting and maintaining 3000 workmen in a remote place far from the centres, against the advantages of cheap raw materials. There is no doubt the new steel company would have its entire plant in before this but for the homesick American workmen.

Stock promotion began in earnest with the plant's founding and the start of construction. Intentionally or not, the newspapers and magazines of the day played an important role in the success of the sale of stock. Politicians took turns prophesying how great Sydney one day would be. In August 1900, Prime Minister Sir Wilfred Laurier said that Sydney "would become not only the Pittsburgh of Canada, but the Glasgow and Belfast of Canada." Federal Finance Minister Fielding and Nova Scotia's Premier Murray came through the next month with praise for the promoters and the plant. J. B. Longley of the Nova Scotia Legislature said in England, "British capitalists should interest themselves in this great development."

Sydney Post, April 27, 1901:

The number of people in Sydney and elsewhere in Cape Breton that are now investing in steel and coal stocks is surprisingly large and includes men in every walk of life, and it is said not a few women.... The craze appears to be prevalent here as well as it is in Montreal and Toronto, where speculators have simply gone wild over these stocks.

While the act of incorporation had Americans in control, within a year the directorate had enlarged with substantial Canadian representation, and the bulk of the money from stock promotion was generated in Canada.

As commercial and construction interests turned toward Sydney, the town and the island were featured in periodicals such as *Canadian Trade Review*, *Canadian Mining Journal*, and the *Gripsack*, a traveling salesmen's publication. The Halifax *Chronicle Herald*'s two-page map of the island was entitled "Land of Boundless Wealth, whose vast mineral riches are commanding the attention of the capitalists of the world."

Sydney was portrayed not only as the site of Canada's greatest industrial development, but as the reasonable centre of the world of trade. The *Gripsack* published a table showing the distances between Sydney, Pittsburgh, and Birmingham, Alabama, and their various markets. In all cases, Sydney proved closest. C. W. Vernon published in his *Cape Breton, Canada* a map depicting Sydney as a world centre. He wrote:

The location and characteristics of Cape Breton are indeed very similar in many respects to those of Great Britain.... The one is possibly at the very zenith of her commercial and maritime supremacy. The other but sees in dim outline the imperial destiny that nature and Providence have in reserve for her.

Meanwhile, Sydney was trying to cope with the reality of the Boom. The *Baddeck Telephone* published letters home from Victoria County people:

The town is besieged by people looking for board and lodging or a house to let. Any kind of a shack will rent for 12 or 15 dollars per month, while houses of the better class cannot be had.

Views from the Steel Plant

So great is the volume of freight arriving at the sheds in Sydney, that it takes four days before you can get your stuff after it arrives....

The mild weather favours building operations, and buildings are going up right and left. If ice should prevent vessels arriving during the next month, there will be a lumber famine. You had better advise your farming friends to stir up the hens, for eggs are retailing at 25 cents per dozen....

Anyone familiar with old Sydney and visiting it today, will scarcely recognize it. It appears as if some booming Western town had been dropped bodily on the site of Sydney, not covering it entirely, but leaving some of the old town protruding through.

In one way the new regime has had a depressing effect on the older citizens. Once the habitue of the street knew every other citizen, and nodded a friendly recognition or stopped for a chat. Now he has to elbow his way through a crowd of strange faces, with a feeling that he is a stranger in the haunts of his youth.

Another wrote his "first impressions of the Iron Age":

In the first place there are lots of people going by, and the procession comprises directors of banks, merchants, speculators, house-hunters, shoals of sharks, armies of mechanics, gangs of labourers—speaking the gibberish of many lands—and the usual camp following of tramps and bums.

The banks have monopolized the corners, and stand like Wisdom of old, calling to the multitudes to cease the pursuit of vanity and deposit their surplusage at $3^1/_2$ per cent.

But in that transformed square mile across the creek, where capital is being dumped by the cart load, there is the exposition of modern enterprise that makes the eyes of rustics like myself stick out till you could hang your hat on them. Five [actually 4] great furnaces—two of them completed—are steadily rising from the blueberry turf.... A train of 150 cars would be necessary to carry away the product of one day's operations....

Will this last? I have no doubt it will, and for this reason: there seems to be an entire absence of that splurge and sputter, marking capital wasted, in a new and untried adventure. The whole thing moves on as if directed by a staff of trained veterans; there are none of the jerky operations always noted in new enterprises conducted by raw recruits.

42

Not unexpectedly, housing remained a serious problem throughout this period—houses, cottages, and tenements for every class—and despite "a perfect revelry of housebuilding," construction constantly lagged behind demand. The newspapers recognized that a problem like this could kill the Boom and tried to encourage local investment in more housing. One reported:

1900 is a record year.... Upward of 560 deeds were recorded.... It is believed that over 400 structures were completed or were under construction during the past year. [That was just not enough.] The older part of Sydney is rapidly filling up...[and] property prices are high. Perhaps the greater number of new buildings have been erected in what is called the Whitney Pier suburb, where in all directions new houses for workmen are meeting with ready sale. Colby, Ashby, and Brooklands, only a year ago farms, are now rapidly building up.... [But in January 1901:] Extensive as operations have been, there is still an unsupplied demand for dwellings. Rents asked for stores and dwellings are abnormally high.... [February 9, 1901:] The question of high rents and scarce houses is one which is seriously affecting the prosperity of Sydney. We have already a large number of skilled mechanics who would settle here and become tax-paying citizens and contributors to the general mercantile concerns...if they could procure houses for their families.... We cannot but deem it unfortunate, to say the least, that more of our moneyed men are not endeavouring to seek the good investment which it is certain that tenement houses are in Sydney today. [Again, on February 25:] There is a lamentable lack of enterprise, and both the town and those who are in a position to take advantage of the boom are the losers thereby. [Construction continued.] Houses are going up in places where the streets are as yet on paper. On the other hand, there are some new streets opened up and graded, awaiting the first house...

But it still did not meet the needs. The daily press was finally exasperated: "Why don't some of our bloated capitalists step in and relieve the situation?"

Both the lack of adequate housing in Sydney, and its high cost, made for crowded, unsanitary conditions. By mid-1900: "Sickness of one kind or another is very prevalent at present in Sydney.... People should be on their guard, especially against typhoid fever." And again: "There is reason to believe that unless radical steps are soon taken, Sydney will have on its hands some very serious problems." The newspapers wanted laws enforced and a careful system of scavenging—garbage pickup—implemented. But the problems were still there in mid-1901: "It is the duty of any town to see that individuals are not allowed to put up shacks where human beings will have to live day after day paying enormous rent, and at the same time leaving their lives foreshortened...."

Dr. Johnson reported to the Board of Health:

In the pier and coke oven districts the boarding houses were overcrowded, beds were being constantly slept in, and night workmen turning in as soon as the day workers got up. Typhoid patients must surely die if left in crowded boarding houses.

A Dr. MacIntyre commented on the inadequate means the town had of cleaning out back yards and privies, and recommended the town hire a man and a number of horses and carts for this work of scavenging. Put simply, garbage was thrown into the streets, the pipes from most houses ran into the streets, and much of the available drinking water was contaminated.

Sufficient water, if not its purity, was a concern from the very beginning, being an element in the town's "encouragement" to the Steel Plant. The company built its own dam to assure a supply. The town continued to grow beyond the capacity of the town fathers to meet its needs. It was difficult for them to find labour, competing as they were with work at the Steel Plant. They advertised for months for 100 labourers to dig needed sewer lines. When a contingent of 30 Russian Jews applied for the trenching job they were turned down as "undesirable, and as far as possible...Cape Breton labour should be engaged." The next summer was dry, but the city engineer said, "There is not the slightest danger of a water famine.... Under our arrangements with the steel company we can have our reservoirs refilled whenever [the water] falls below a certain level."

By October 10, 1901: "Sydney has been supplied altogether by the steel company." They were trying to both repair the town's dam and clear its reservoir, "but the town is embarrassed for want of men and horses. We have advertised for men and horses and cannot get a third of what is wanted to hurry the work to completion."

At the same time, Mayor Crowe pointed out that he didn't

44

think water had anything to do with high insurance rates, that there was plenty of water for domestic use and for fighting fires. Still:

the insurance companies have borne hard on Sydney but I am told the town is partly to blame. We were told to proclaim a brick district [a kind of fire wall] before the boom got well underway, but met with a little sympathy from most citizens...affected.... We have now a fire limit which prohibits the erection of any but brick and stone buildings between Dorchester and Wentworth streets. [This decision seems to have been made only in the previous few days—it was resisted on the basis of cost and inconvenience, and a smaller district than first desired was proclaimed. Certainly nothing had been built under this new decision. The mayor continued:] Meantime, however, some buildings which are no better than firetraps have been built on this street, with the result that insurance in those blocks is hard to get and very expensive.

Not ten days later the headlines read: "TODAY'S BLAZE The Most Disastrous Fire in the History of Sydney"—The Great Sydney Fire of October 19, 1901. [See photos of the aftermath of the fire on pages 46 and 47.]

An insurance man called it "hardly unexpected," and pointed out that every new house connected to the water lines tended to "weaken the force." The newspaper insisted it wasn't true that for two hours of the fire "there was 'not a drop of water.'" The mayor tried to explain: the reservoir was *not* dry and it was not true the steel company's main was cut off for repairs. Actually, "the water had been turned off between Wentworth and Pitt Streets for the purpose of making a connection—an event that might occur at any time."

Two days later the town worked out a water deal with the steel company. The company was to furnish nine million gallons a year at $400. Any extra would cost $4^1/_2$ cents every thousand gallons. The company would pay $10 for the meter.

Wooden buildings were not the only way in which the structure of Sydney was vulnerable. One day a man named Ryan came to town. He lounged around, said little, people watched him. He gave a few hints. Next day he was gone. The headlines rumoured that J. P. Morgan's syndicate had taken over the steel company. The *Daily*

The Great Fire in Sydney—October 19, 1901

Start of the fire

View from Prince Street

Another view from Prince Street

Charlotte Street from Prince Street

Charlotte Street from Wentworth

Charlotte Street, west side, Wentworth to Prince

Record tried to keep a lid on Sydney, but the panic showed through. It seemed reasonable that Morgan would want DISCO, especially after Moxham's extraordinary speech before the Canadian Manufacturing Association at the Board of Trade in Toronto. Moxham— vice-president and general manager of the company—said, regarding Pittsburgh steel which was then controlling the world market, "after careful checking of his figures he found that Cape Breton could export steel to Europe at $6 per ton less than Pittsburgh. This gave the company control of the export trade."

The *Daily Record* rammed the point home: "This means that Cape Breton will control the market of the world...."

The Toronto *Globe* called Moxham's speech "sound as it was undoubtedly in the best sense sensational." But the *Industrial Advocate* said, "It must be confessed that we do not share Mr. Moxham's opinion that his plant can produce iron at a price so greatly below that of other famous districts...."

But Sydney believed it. And that's where the rumour of the takeover broke out: "EXTRA — Steel Deal Accomplished — The Morgan trust now controls the plant.... At 5 p.m. on Saturday the deal was completed.... It was given out by Mr. Ryan and is without doubt authentic." Interviews with various commercial people in Sydney drew assurances that it made no difference, the plant would probably continue, there was no need for alarm. But there clearly was alarm. Again and again, via letter and telegram and in interviews, Whitney had to assure Sydney he had not abandoned them.

By the next day the *Daily Record* had recovered its accustomed composure and scolded local readers for the "mild panic in which Sydney threw itself yesterday "over the 'Alleged Morgan-Whitney Deal.' We are reminded of the harmful predictions that heralded Mr. Whitney's investment in the coal business in 1893.... The coal mines were to be sold at once to Pennsylvania 'coal barons' and closed up.... Mr. Whitney and the men associated with him were freely denounced as 'freebooters,' 'robbers,' and 'blowhards.'... The predictions were each and all jointly and severally falsified by the event, and everybody now recognizes that the real industrial development of Cape Breton dates from the 'crime of 1893' [creation of the Dominion Coal Company]. The blue ruin bogeyman cannot be worked today. That ghost will not walk."

But it *did* walk, and the next day: "Timid people are still in a state of alarm." The paper reminded readers that Whitney said, "(1) that there is no foundation for the report and (2) that the businessmen of Sydney need have no fear of anything being done that will interfere with the fullest development of the iron and steel business in Sydney and make it a great industrial centre. We are thus assured by Mr. Whitney that in any event the interests of Sydney will be safeguarded."

A real estate agent denied the Halifax *Herald*'s report that property in Sydney had slumped 25% because of the "Ryan episode and rumoured steel transfer.... The *Herald* correspondent's other statement, namely that many merchants had cancelled their spring orders for goods, appears to be equally unfounded."

But the nervousness was still in the air.

The rumour of Morgan's takeover broke out twice more in 1901. It never actually happened. And the press was always there to counter that threat or, in fact, any hint that the Boom was over.

Meanwhile, the new Steel Plant itself had come to life. The headline read:

FLAME APPLIED

At 8:30 on the evening of Saturday, February 2nd, 1901, "the slumbering energies" were awakened in the blast furnace of the Dominion Iron and Steel Company, and heat for the first time applied to those monsters of production which will yield the first manufactured iron in the history of Cape Breton. The ceremony was simple and quiet—in fact it may be said there was an absence of ceremony altogether.

The modern method was followed in charging the furnace. An immense altar of wood was built at the base, upon which was piled a quantity of blank coke, and then in regular order and proportion stratas of coke, iron ore and limestone. This fabric being completed, Miss Edith Gettings, sister by adoption of Mr. McCreary, superintendent of the works, applied the first match, and the flame leaped merrily....

As to what hour and date the first product of pig iron would appear, [McCreary] stated that it depended altogether upon conditions, and that the present state of the atmosphere was unfavourable to rapid production.... [He] was safe in hoping that by Tuesday afternoon at the latest the crucible would be tapped.

[February 6th they reported the first cast of pig iron.] In that product is the budding materialization of the hopes and efforts of the gentlemen who have invested their capital in the mighty enterprise, and of the citizens of Sydney who have encouraged its establishment.

The crowning incident of the day was the crowning of the molten iron. This work, which was witnessed by quite a number of people, was not accomplished without much labor and danger, not only to the workmen but to the spectators as well. After the bar was driven well in, it was by relays of muscular young men, who wielded huge sledgehammers, withdrawn. A sudden flash, a sullen roar, and the hoarse shouts of the men proclaimed the "open door." Out rushed the molten mass, and within the space, probably of a minute, the moulds or pigs fronting the furnace were filled.

"I've seen worse results than that," remarked Mr. Moxham to Mr. Coffin.

"Yes, very much," replied the gentleman addressed.

By February 11 Sydney was told that Mr. Whitney "is pleased as a boy with a new sled over the success of the first casting of pig iron."

By the end of summer 1901, the major portion of the construction phase of the Steel Plant was over. S. T. Woods wrote for the *Toronto Globe*:

Although the work of construction is by no means completed, and steel-making will not be underway before October, the change from a construction to a working force is already felt. The great capacious dining hall of the company stands like an abandoned skating rink, and the long row of buildings in which the army of construction workers were housed is almost empty. Many of the former occupants and patrons have taken up their residence in the town, but many more have finished their work and gone elsewhere.

By December 1901, the first steel was poured. Both Whitney and Moxham had left the steel company. James Ross was the new president and control was firmly in Central Canadian financial hands.

Whitney and Moxham would be accused of "reckless and extravagant expenditure and miscalculation," and that they were as "extravagant in building the plant as in talking of it." Don MacGillivray's 1980 article on Whitney pointed out: "A rail mill was partially erected and then discarded and replaced by another type. Considerable expense was incurred before it was realized that the type of ore was unsuitable to the Bessemer process." It was said that between seven and eight million dollars was wasted and the entire plant could have been built for two-thirds the cost. By 1903 *Canadian Mining Review* was writing about the "Dark Hour of Dominion Iron and Steel Company."

But that was not the end of it. It was hardly the beginning. Whitney and Moxham left behind Sydney, three times the population of what it had been and a third of what it would become—although it would never reach the Boom estimates of up to 75,000. They left behind wage-paying jobs in what many considered a state-of-the-art plant, where "electricity was used in every conceivable way," having "done away with nearly all the hard, exposing, brutalizing labour." But there are others who insist that the plant was poorly built, that the coal and iron ore were never satisfactory, and the entire operation was established as a stock scam.

In any case, they left behind Sydney, described in Summer 1901 by Mark Sullivan, *Boston Transcript*, as:

a perfect type of boom town of the West planted here on the northeastern tip of Cape Breton Island...redolent with the smell of cheap pine timber and fresh paint, and every second building on Main Street a "dry goods emporium," and the ones between real estate offices...25 miles of country roads that go by the name of city streets because they form rectangles, streets in which you wade ankle deep in mud or dust...for there is scarcely a yard of sidewalk; 3000 cheap frame houses, those that are finished crowded till the windows bulge with labourers and their families, half that are still building filled with families before the roof is on—and for all those houses no sewerage except the few miles that is just now being laid, the trenches and the uncovered terra cotta adding their mite to the general ugliness and unkemptness...an esplanade lined with cheap boarding houses and 3-room "hotels,"..."the finest courthouse in eastern Canada" finished to the foundations; newspapers whose daily text is "the marvellous strides of progress made by our beautiful city in the past 6 months"; pretentious iron railings that enclose what here passes for a fine residence, joining with a rail "worm" fence that encloses a cow pasture in the middle of the city; ...such is Sydney today.

December 31, 1901: "First steel made in Cape Breton...poured last night. Quality of steel in every way excellent.... This steel means another product of Cape Breton placed on the markets of the world, and the bringing into existence of a commercial commodity that is destined to revolutionize trade relations in these parts of Canada."

CHAPTER 3

From Conversations with Steelworkers

How Mike Oleschuk Got His Farm

MIKE OLESCHUK: I was born in Austria. Then after the war, it became occupied and called the Ukraine. And then in 1918-19 the Polish occupied it. And with the Polish passport I came to Canada. But my nationality is Ukrainian.

I came to Canada in 1929—May 31—I landed in Quebec. I came there to be on a farm. See, in the Old Country I had two sisters, and we had there only 12 acres of land. And I didn't want to work like a slave. I could see what would happen. I'd get married and my father would split up the piece of land—a piece for one sister, a piece for another sister, piece of land for me—and after, I'll have nothing to give my children. In the Old Country, some people ended up working for landlords all their lives. That's all they had. But I did not want to work like a slave. And that's what made me decide to sell my land and pay my fare and come away to Canada.

Okay. I came to Canada. I brought all my money—$1200. That

time that was quite a lot of money. I didn't know one word of English. And those agents get you, you don't know—took me to where there were bushes and bushes everywhere. I got a homestead and nobody there. I was by myself. Lots of Ukrainians came to that area, but everybody was around, living far away from one another. I found a farm—80 acres cleared land, a house was built up with logs. It was nice, three rooms—$3000. I was satisfied. I gave down $1000. Now I've got to work and pay it up—$2000, that's the mortgage. All those neighbours there said, "Don't worry." They said, "In a couple more years there you'll be cleared up. Don't worry...." But my grain stays there. I can't sell it. What's the good? Mortgage combined with interest, interest. I went working for 50 cents a day, cleaning up their land, other people's land—what's the 50 cents a day? How am I going to make the payments?

Well, I started looking around every place there to find a better job—no job. And I had a brother-in-law living here in Sydney. And before I left the Old Country, he was sending money to his wife in the Old Country. She bought land, built a nice home. He was in Sydney. He worked in the Steel Plant. I wrote him a letter. I said, "Look, I would like to come to Sydney." He wrote, "Don't come, because there's nothing here." He said, "I'm working only one shift in a month, one furnace going—that's all. Only one furnace." I don't want to believe it. Because how did that happen there in two years—so quick? Well, I said, there's something fishy. He doesn't want me there. I decided to go. I met a fellow—a Ukrainian guy, but he was born in Ontario and he talked Ukrainian and he had good English. That's good for me, you know, anything I'd want to know, I could find out in my language. He was my buddy.

Well, we became hobos right through to Sydney on the train. Sometimes the police chased me out but, well, you catch another one. That's the way I landed in Sydney. One morning, the boxcar landed in the yard there in Sydney. We woke up to the stink from the Steel Plant. We got up, opened the door—I looked and, by jeez, there's *lots* of stacks. I said, oh, we'll get a job here. A big factory. Oh by gosh.

Well, we get up, go and wash ourselves with the stinky water there by the brook, and we go to Number 1 Gate. Nobody stopped us. We landed in the Bar Mill. By gosh, I could see lots of butts there, cigarette butts. We saw nobody there, so we picked up those butts, made a smoke. Then we walked. Didn't see anybody. We came back and I go back to the gate and I asked the fellows there, "Where's the Whitney Pier?" And they told me where to go.

Well, we came to the Pier. I asked, "Where's my brother-in-law, anybody know?" Well, they sent me to another fellow with the same name. I found him and I see that's not my brother-in-law. But he called me into the house, gave us something to eat. And he gave us each a package of tobacco. And he told me to go to Edel Hirsh on Lingan Road, that all the foreigners deal there. Ukraine, Polish, Hungarian, Italian deal there. It's a grocery store. He speaks Ukraine, Polish, all kind of languages—he's an Old Country Jew. So: "Yeah," he said, "he deals here in my store. He lives on Henry Street."

I go there and a lady hollers up, there's somebody to see him. Right away I'm recognized. We shake hands and everything. He asks me questions: how I landed, how did everything go there. Sat down and talked. I told him all the history. He asked me about his wife and children in the Old Country and how are things there. "Well," he said, "Mike, there's nothing here in Sydney." He's saved a few dollars, and he had to pay the board for me. I saw, by gosh, I've got to go looking for something. A fellow had a farm at Blackett's Lake; he wanted someone to clear up the land. Well, I went there with my buddy, the Canadian-born fellow I came with to Sydney.

"Yeah, I could take you both." We've got a job. I don't ask him how much he pays because I am glad to have some place to sleep and something to eat. Well, he paid us 25 cents a day, and board. And we slept in the barn. That was summer. That was okay. And I was a good worker. And every Saturday he goes with the eggs and everything to town—and every Saturday he bought me tobacco, half a pound—but none for my buddy. I think that's because he'd go away and his wife would watch what I do. And when I work, I work. If I want to smoke, that's the only time I stop.

We worked there for pretty near four months—25 cents a day. And it was in September, a hot day, and my buddy sat down by a tree and took a snooze. And the farmer's wife watched. He came home in the evening and his wife told him—says Mike is working, and that fellow sat down and was asleep. He told my buddy to go. "If you want to stay, Mike, you can stay. And I'll give you 50 cents a day." I worked one more week. Then one day my buddy walked out to Blackett's Lake, eight miles. He said, "Mike, a boat came to load pulp. I put your name there. Thirty dollars a month and board." I had just got 50 cents a day. By gosh, now I had a dollar a day. I'll be a millionaire. And we went there and we loaded pulp. We worked there three months before it froze and we quit. Well, I made $90. I was a rich man.

After that, relief was open to us. And we had to go to City Hall and "carry the bag." We had to go from Whitney Pier to Sydney and register for the relief, and we had to go there every Wednesday, go pick up our groceries. Give you the codfish, turnips, two loaves of bread—a dollar's worth. That was relief at that time. This was not only Ukrainians. English people were doing this, too. Didn't make any difference what you were—it's the '30s and nobody's working.

In 1933 I got married to a Canadian-born girl, and jobs started to pick up, the Steel Plant started to pick up a little bit. Open Hearth got four furnaces and Blast Furnace got one furnace—and I tried to get a job. My wife was working with Mrs. Melnick in the store, and Mrs. Melnick told her there's going to be an opening at the coal bank, a job dumping coal. "Only thing," my wife told me, "you've got to give the foreman a bottle of rum." And I said, "Where would I get the money to buy the bottle?" And I had to give him the bottle to *get* the job. *And* you had to be lucky. You had to have, beside the rum, that Mrs. Melnick *knows* him. If she didn't know him, I wouldn't get the job even if I had the rum.

My wife went to Mrs. Melnick, and Mrs. Melnick bought a bottle of rum and gave it to her. And I took the rum and got a job. Only thing, to *actually* work, it has to be a stormy day because the boss had lots of friends. He gave the work first to his friends. There was no such a thing as you go there in the morning and go to work. He says, "Okay, go pick up the shovel there—you, you, you, you, you, go pick up." I've got to stay back. If he takes me, okay. If he doesn't take me, I'll have to go back home. (*Even though now you have a job?*) Yeah, I have a job. I gave him the rum and he gave me a job. But each day I've got to go there. If he wants me to work that day, he picks me. If he doesn't want me, he doesn't pick me. (*And you do get paid if you don't get picked?*) No. (*And that's the job you have.*) That's the job I have. And if the weather is bad, some of the fellows don't come out. Lots of times, I prayed that they'd have bad weather so I could get a shift.

(*And what was the job you were lucky enough to get?*) A loaded train comes out on the bank of coal, and you've got to take the coal off. The last cars, maybe the last 10 cars, you had it easy—you open the door and the coal falls down the bank by itself. They could be dumped. But if you're by the engine, you've got to shovel every piece of coal, because you're far away from the edge of the bank. (*And which cars did you get?*) I'd have the cars by the engine. I had to shovel the coal out of the car and over the bank, every time.

Hard work. And dirty work. And those times, for us there was no such a thing as a bathtub, sink—you had to bring a bucket inside to wash yourself—and coal is dirty. You had to clean up. Only

the work clothes that I used, I put aside, and in the morning I'd put them on—so I'd get dirty again, before I'd go. If I worked or didn't work—when I came back, I'd be dirty and have to wash again. I'd be dirty anyhow. And lots of times I had to come back without working. I'd only get to work in the worse weather—snowing, blowing, rain—that's the day I'd get a job. (*And your pay?*) Twenty-eight cents an hour. That was good money, that time. I made $2.80 a day. And if I'd work a whole day there, I'd come home and get something to eat and wash myself, and you could say there was music, there was dancing—I didn't care. I was beat. And I was young. I was young and I was beat.

(*How much coal would you shovel in a shift?*) Oh, the small cars, two men could shovel 10 cars in a day—that's 15 tons in a car. That's in a shift when an engine was always there, you could shovel up to 10 cars, that's 10 trips. Some days it would be eight trips, five trips. But if you had two engines going, you could get 10 cars. You were supposed to be working 10 hours, but sometimes it would get dark and you'd only get eight hours. (*So even into the '30s, you were working those long days.*) Oh yeah. And some days you'd work 24 hours [when you changed your shift to day shift or day shift to night]—you stayed 24 hours in the Steel Plant. They'd give you an hour to go home, take your lunch, and go back. Only you never worked on the coal bank at nighttime.

(*That sounds like a rough job.*) People do it. I did it. (*Was this the kind of job you'd only give to people from the Old Country?*) Oh no, no such a thing there. Canadian-born people too. They were fair on that. Only generally, the foreign peoples had to *buy* the job, like I told you. (*A bottle of rum to get the job.*) Well, if you wanted to work steady in Sydney, you had to give the boss a bottle every week. He forgets that first bottle. There even was an agent in the Open Hearth and the mixer—he collected two dollars from each one there and gave it to the boss, so those fellows could stay on the job. The bosses had the power that time. No union. What place could you go? The foremen controlled the whole thing. If you're in good with the foreman, okay, you could be working. In 1933, my father-in-law was working in the big plant. And he told the foreman to take me there in the spring, take me to make brick. So I got that job.

From Conversations with Steelworkers

You have a tank there and a chute and molds, and you have to beat mud, and beat it good so you don't have a rock—so that it will be solid and smooth. You work with another man who picks up the bricks and puts them onto a car to go to the kiln. After the fellows there took them out, the bricks went to the Open Hearth and the blast furnaces and other places they used it in the plant.

(*Was it easier than working on the coal bank?*) Didn't make any difference at the Steel Plant what you did—it was a hard job. Making brick, you've got to work like a son-of-a-gun—4-by-9, you've got to make 2000 bricks; and slab brick, 9-by-10, you've got to make about 1200 to 1400 for each car. You made four, five, six cars a day—there was no contract on that. And they paid you by the hour. Stripper had 28 cents an hour, and mold man working at the beater there, he had 30 cents an hour.

(*You must have been tired all the time.*) I was young. You get a little bit of rest, and you forget. And no such a thing as a union. You talk about union, and you're out. (*So you didn't talk about unions?*) Well, I talked. But you've got to know to whom you talk. You watch for the progressive people who know what is what. If you figure there is danger, you don't talk about those things. I was two years, and all summers I made the brick. And in the wintertime we'd go there in the General Yard. I worked with the bricklayers. I carried the brick with the wheelbarrow. (*What were bricks used for?*) Used it for the furnace, used it for what the gas goes through, it's called the checkers. Gas goes through the checkers to the furnace to melt the steel, coming from the gas producers. The clay bricks from Scotland and other countries, they go in the checkers. The bricks that I made here in Sydney, they went to line the furnaces—in the roof and the sides of the furnace. I helped line the furnace.

And if the furnace is hot—that's a hard job there again. If the furnace has got to go through a repair, put the new brick there, you've got to go in there with bars and break the old brick out. Then you go into the furnace and you line it. (*Did they turn the furnace off, let it cool down before you go in?*) Oh, no, no. Not too cool. Sometimes hot, by jeez. But the boss said go, and there was no union that time—if he told you to go, you put a wet bag over your head and go in there. The wet bag is so you don't burn yourself. Your shoes—you're working two shifts there, you don't have shoes. You climb into the furnace. You can't stay in too long. The heat chokes you. You go in for as long as you can stand. Pick up the bricks and throw them away outside. Pick up the bricks and throw them away—pick up as much as you can there. After they see you choking and your back steaming where you put the wet bag over your head—you get out and another fellow's got to go in. (*Terrible job.*) I know that. And no union to protect you. The boss said, you go in. And you'd have to come early to get a shift—wait maybe an hour and a half—the boss would check you in—and sometimes not. And if you don't get a shift that day, you go home, no pay. No such thing as a guarantee that you have a shift. No sir. (*And when you had the old brick out?*) The bricklayers and helpers go in there and line the furnace again.

And after 1935 I changed my number to the Open Hearth. There were slag pockets, and you have to take that slag out. Sometimes it was so hard, you're jigging and jigging with the air hammer and you only get a little piece. I go with the air hammer, and the other fellows shovel up into the boxes, and I go again with the air hammer. You've got to break it, and they shovel it into boxes and the train picks it up and takes it away. After that, I was millwright for a while. And when I retired I was in the brick—lining the ladles for the steel. I retired in 1970. I worked 39 years at the Steel Plant.

And I was always active. In 1936 we went for a union. We made a start. We called a mass meeting and people were scared. Only seven of us landed there in the CCF hall in the Pier. But we finally got organized and got the legislation, and we got the check-off. [See "The Coming of the Trade Union Act, 1937," Chapter 5.] And the union bargained from 10 hours to the eight-hour day.

And I was active in 1948, I was involved. The Seamen's Union came out on strike, tied up the ore boat. And Corbett was president of 1064, called me up. I was on the Grievance Committee, represented all the workers there on the Open Hearth. We went to a meeting in Glace Bay. Jenkins was there. He represented the miners. And we decided, what are we going to do with the Seamen's Union? And it was solid—miners and steelworkers would support

Men working in cooled-down Open Hearth furnace

them. And we discussed that we needed a place to put them up. We had a labour temple hall on Mount Pleasant Street, and Jenkins and Corbett asked me if I would give the labour temple hall for the Seamen's Union to stay. I can't give it because we had at that time 90 members, and the members own that hall.

Next day I called the meeting of our members, Ukrainian Benefit Society. I explained what the struggle was, and our members, nearly every one, were for the union—it was a progressive organization, you know what I mean. The motion was agreed—give the hall for the seamen to stay there, cook there, go on the picket line. And we supported them—oh, over three months. Miners supported them. They even came from New Waterford and Glace Bay for the picket line. And the steelworkers went and helped them there on the picket line.

But then propaganda was started that this Seamen's Union was a communist union, all kinds of stuff that put the bogeyman to the people. And next Sunday priests and ministers said, if those people stay out and we don't have the ore, the plant would be closed down. And the trouble started. And local boys were in the Seamen's Union.

The steelworkers had a mass meeting. One fellow stepped up and told all the steelworkers there that we've got to look after ourselves, it's a communist union—if the plant goes down where will we go? There was a meeting, and some said, "Go out and beat them." Anyhow, they went down and broke up the Seamen's Union picket line. And at that time, even miners from Glace Bay and New Waterford were on the picket line. Chased them away. And that broke the Seamen's Union strike.

And because I supported the Seamen's Union and my wife made sandwiches for the picket line and everything—some even said, "Go burn Mike Oleschuk's house." The committee stopped them, said if I wanted to support them, it was my idea.

Well, Jack Moraff, the Jew, he was my good friend. He didn't work at the plant but he was a good progressive man, and he knew me well. He came the next day. He said, "Mike, you have small children. By jeez, if you get kicked out of that plant, what are you going to do?" I said I didn't know. He said, "You saw what happened to Forlett—he had to go to the Old Country. He got blacklisted and he can't get citizen papers and he can't get a damned thing—this'll be happening to you." He said, "Quit that. Let the Canadian people do it. You're a foreigner." I said, "Jack, I can't do it. It's too late for me." I said, "What the hell am I going to do?" He said, "Buy a piece of land and go there and farm there. If you get a kick in the ass, at least you can make a living." "How can I buy a piece of land?" "Don't worry. You're my good friend, and if you'd like to go on the farm—I'll buy it."

And that's the way I landed on the farm. He took the mortgage. The farm cost $10,000 and I paid $10,000.

I paid only for the bank administration, two dollars a year for 18 years. So I paid $36 interest for $10,000. You could say that was a good friend? He didn't make anything. An Old Country Jew. I'd come home from the Steel Plant and work the farm. We had cows—10 cows at that time—and horses, pigs, chickens, garden—everything there. I'm coming on 74. I fought, and I'm still fighting. And you could say the Seamen's Union and Jack Moraff finally put me there on the farm.

1919 overview of the Coke Ovens, Dominion Iron and Steel Company, seen from the pushers' side. These were still in use through World War Two.

Regarding the Coke Ovens

J. T. COLLIER, *Manager of Coke Ovens*: Of course, the Coke Plant is only the very beginning of the steel process. That makes coke which is used as a fuel, also chemically to smelt iron ore into iron in the Blast Furnace. From there the hot iron is taken to the Open Hearth and made into steel. Coke has nothing to do with that.

Today [1979] coal for coke comes from selected mines—but when I went

63

there first, it was all Cape Breton coal. Cape Breton coal makes a very poor coke. It's very very high volatile and it runs about 35 or 36 per cent volatile, and the reaction is so violent that it makes a very friable coke that will not support the burden in the Blast Furnace. You want good burden so you can get a draft through all the time. [Cape Breton coal] breaks down and causes plugging. So for that reason, we selectively blend coals, blending coals that are less volatile with the high volatile coals locally, and end up with a composite that's probably around 29 per cent volatile. By volatile, I mean the gaseous stuff that's actually driven off during the coking process.

(*So you don't want the coke to actually catch fire?*) Well, the coke is made in a sealed chamber. It can't catch fire. There's no air in there. A coke oven is a literal name—coal is baked in an oven. Behind those doors are brick chambers that are hermetically sealed, are under pressure, and are heated from without, just like an oven. You bake coal just like you bake bread—you don't burn it, you bake it, to get coke. You can get by-products from the gas. But your primary purpose in the coke plant is to make a fuel for the Blast Furnace. That's your reason for existence. Anything else, any by-product, is incidental.

About 40 per cent of the gas we extract is used to heat the Coke Ovens—that's where they get their heat from, their own gas. (*The gas that comes off goes right back to the oven?*) Yes. It is used to continue the heating process. When we built the new plant [1949], we used gas from the old plant to get it heated up—till it got hot enough to put coal in it. Then it becomes self-supporting. If we hadn't had gas, we would have had to heat it some way—wood fires or propane or some other way. You heat your oven up just once in its life—then you operate it till it's finished. You never shut it down till it's worn out. (*How long might its life be?*) Well, the present battery was built in 1949. It was heated up in 1949. (*This is 1979, and it has never cooled down?*) That's right. (*And it runs itself by the gases that come off the coal.*) That's right.

(*Coal goes in, the oven is sealed....*) And the gas, the volatile is driven off, under pressure so you don't get danger of fire in there that could cause an explosion—big extractors draw the gas away

64

from the ovens. Tar is a by-product. It precipitates out at atmospheric temperatures, so that's easy to extract. Then you cool the gas, wash and treat it—send it through an oil tower where the light oil in the gas is absorbed. Then after that, you're through with it. You send it back to the ovens as fuel, and the balance is boosted to the steel mills for use in the mills.

You bring the new coke oven up to temperature—that takes anywhere from 7 to 9 weeks to heat it up originally. We start with the ovens themselves, until the temperature of the brick is such that it's incandescent and will light the gas. Then we go into the flues. It's safe to go into the flues then because if it doesn't ignite, it's going to build up a pocket of gas and explode. You want the gas to light instantly. In 1949 we had a new oven. Internally it was all silica brick. And it's surrounded by either metal or clay brick, and it's all held together in a steel grid-like, and that's it.

The coke oven is built cold, naturally, and once it heats, it grows, it gets bigger—and that expansion has got to be controlled. So when they build the thing, to control its expansion, there are certain places they allow to move, and they put what are called slip joints in. Holding it together with springs and wooden blocks are other means of controlling it until it's fully grown. Because when it's at the heating temperature it's got to be at the right elevation— because you've built a whole lot of sensitive machinery at a certain elevation and it has got to be absolutely true. It heats up and grows longer and wider and higher—gradually heating it up to its proper temperature. (*Which produces at the same time a proper size coke oven.*) That's right. It has to line up to the pushing machine, a big ram that goes through the oven and pushes the coke out. (*You place machinery and build it with the idea it will all line up properly only after it's heated.*) That's right.

And you prefer it never to cool down. You'd like to operate at a constant temperature. But because of the ups and downs of the economy you can't always do that, because you don't always need that much coke or you need more than you can make.... So you try to maintain a constant heat—but also you try to heat at what rate the plant is operating.

Actually, the coke oven is a battery—a whole lot of ovens. In

65

our plant there are 114 ovens, two batteries. Each oven is about 40 feet long, average width of 17 inches, about 13 feet high. There are four ports at the top, and a machine goes along with the exact volume of coal to fill that oven—dump the coal in the ovens and replace the lids—and depending on what temperature you're up to, anywhere from 17, 18, to 20 hours later, you come back and push that oven—pushing machine comes along and pushes the ram through the 40-foot length—coked out. The coke is pushed into the quenching car. After it gets the charge of coke, it goes down to the quenching tower and we dump water on it. And that's when you see that plume of steam going up over Sydney.

When the ram comes back, we put the doors back on, do any cleaning up that's needed—and then the oven is charged with coal again. It's probably empty, oh, 20 minutes or so. The heat of the brick carbonizes the new charge of coal. (*And gets it started right away.*) Yes. (*Gives off gases....*) That are processed to some extent, and about 40 per cent of it goes back to burners to continue the heating process.

Lew Allan Davis and the Railroad in the Steel Plant

LEW ALLAN DAVIS: I was born the 12th day of August, 1887. I'll be 92 my birthday [1979]. I was born in Newfoundland. A lot of the people who came to the plant were born there—I suppose 50 per cent at that time. The old tradition was going from Newfoundland to Sydney, going to work. I was 22 when I came to Cape Breton—and the Steel Plant was already going. I hired on there in 1909, just common labouring. You had to work a certain amount of time that way, and if you felt like you were capable of handling another job, you could look for it, and after a while you'd get transferred to that job.

I started railroading. They had 14 or 15 engines there—two shifts—from 6 in the evening to 7 in the morning, and then day shift would start 7 in the morning and quit 6 in the evening. I wasn't operating an engine. I was outside, brakeman at that time. There's a crew, you know. A fireman and an engineer and three men outside—conductor and two brakemen. Well, when you worked yourself up, you'd become a conductor and you had charge of the whole crew. In that kind of work, you know, it's not like on the main line. There were no passengers. The job of the railroad was to tie the plant together.

The conductor, he got the orders and told the men what to do, where to go. Nighttime, you'd get the orders for the whole night, but daytime you'd get so many orders, and then when that was done you'd go back for some more. Say a call would come in from the Open Hearth to make a shunt—so you'd go in there and pull out so many cars. And then you'd have empties to put back. Clear of the steel, all the Open Hearth made was rubbish—slag and dirt and everything. It would be all cleaned up and we'd haul it to the dump. And there'd be 13 or 14 trains going, all going at the same time, all around the plant. Some would be going out to Sydney, to the CNR, and another one would be coming down from the Coke Ovens— haul down 8 or 10 or 15 cars of coke—and that'd go to the Blast Furnace, use that in the Blast Furnace. And when the iron was ready, we'd take that to the Open Hearth—hauling hot metal.

There'd be two engines working at the Open Hearth—running from the stockpile to the Open Hearth—such as limestone, scrap, and ore—that's to feed the furnace. Now when the steel is ready to tap out, a small engine—what they call a narrow gauge—it goes in there and hauls the ladles out. That's steel. It's hauled away and poured into molds—and the bigger train doesn't come along again until it's a finished product, whether it's billets or rails or axle steel—

ship that to Sydney. Perhaps for Montreal, goodness knows where. They'd be hauled generally by the CNR when they're leaving the plant. But when a boat would come in, want to load rails or billets—we'd haul them down to the docks, and we'd haul the ore from the docks. I'll tell you, they were pretty busy there one time.

Those were all steam engines, burning coal. Things were so ancient. They used to have a lot of accidents. (*You hurt your hand....*) Caught between two cars. Cars were coupled up, you know, with link-and-pin. You had to put the link in and drop the pin, and sometimes you'd get caught—pinched. It was common. That was the original equipment over the Old Country. I lost three months for that hand. I got five dollars a week. (*From the company?*) No, from our benefit society—and if we hadn't had a union, I'd have had nothing.

But oh, I've seen accidents there, terrible bad accidents. I know one fellow, he wasn't working on the railroad, but he was walking, crossing the track in the plant. And we were just after having lunch, and there were two engines there in that department. And this engine backed down and the man got out of the way. But he didn't see the next one coming—and it knocked him down—cut him right in two. But oh, I've seen men there would be killed and never had a mark on them. Hit by the train, but the way they fell, you wouldn't see any injuries. Or perhaps stumbled and fell. I knew a man there, when the train backed in, this brakeman wasn't there. So the conductor investigated, walked up the track a piece—there he was on the ground, dead. (*What had happened?*) Goodness knows.

In the early years there were a lot of accidents. There was an accident where the engine coming down way up from what they call the assembly yard—that's where the coal company would put their coal for the Steel Plant. There was a man driving an engine. He had three heavy loads on it. And he was going up this hill, and a train of coal coming down, ran into him. Same track. The driver was killed. That was the night shift. And the fireman, he was lucky, he jumped out. It could be, if the driver had jumped out the same side, he could have got clear—but he didn't.

He went the wrong way and the tender of the engine came up and pinned him against the boiler—he burned to death.

From Conversations with Steelworkers

Oh, there were quite a few accidents. There was a man with his legs off—oh, there's three or four ended with their legs off. And at that time there was very little compensation for anything like that. (*What would a man do, say, if he lost a leg?*) Well, if he'd be able to walk, the company would find a job for him. Perhaps watchman on a gate.

(*In accidents, did they ever spill steel?*) Oh yes, I was on the metal engine one time, and it was daytime and the head ladle—the axle broke. We handled three or four ladles at a time—they were small ones. Axle broke and she tipped over, spilled the whole thing. That would spread right over quite an area, you know. They'd have to break it up. I've seen hot slag that came from the steel—that came in ladles too—and I've seen men burned to death with that.

I was up on the trestle one day, working on the high pier—and there was this explosion right down below us—at the Blast Furnace. And I saw one man coming back. There were two men went up there. But the second man didn't come back. Burned to death. That slag spread, you know. It's almost as bad as the metal. The cause of the explosion would be dampness in the bottom of the ladle, before they poured the slag in it. If it was metal, the ladle wouldn't break because they were made of plate iron. But if it was a slag ladle, it might break because they were made out of cast iron. An explosion would break the ladle, and there's trucks under the ladle, and sometimes the explosion would blow the trucks right from underneath.

Oh, yes. And trains coming off the track. All depends on where you were. If there was another engine handy, they'd get together and pull one on. But they weren't going very fast. You could go as fast as you like on the main line, but in the Steel Plant—in the yard you had a speed limit, 10 or 15 miles an hour. Unless you were trying to get up a grade and you had a heavy load on—then you might go a little faster to try and make it.

We'd go up to the high pier. That's where they'd unload the iron ore for the Blast Furnace. The low pier would be for loading steel. The train itself never went off the pier, but cars have been knocked over. Another train coming and the cars in the way—she'd knock the cars off the track, over the pier. (*Into the water?*) No.

69

There was so much landing before you'd come to the water. And people fell off the pier. And I remember a man, he went over the pier *on* a car. A long time ago. Killed.

(*And wasn't there a train, a shunter, known as "The Man-killer"?*) Yes—125. And she had a screechy whistle. You heard it and it would go through you. And this engine had killed quite a few. I don't know why. It just happened that way. There was no reason for it, in a way. Nothing wrong with the engine. And nothing wrong with the man that was driving it. But that's the way. It had run people over. Man would be working on a track and this engine would come by and hit him. (*Considering the noise, aren't you surprised that people would get hit by trains?*) Yes. But that happens yet.

And in the wintertime, there'd be a lot of snow around the plant—and at that early time, no equipment to handle it. But finally they got a sweeper—and that connects on to the engine, run by steam. (*Before that?*) Well, we just plowed through it the best way you can.

I've seen us out there nights and nights, couldn't make a move with snow. The Steel Plant would have to slow up. And they'd buck the snow, buck the snow, one engine after another, try to get where they were going—and finally they'd get there. Hard work. We could shovel if we wanted—everybody did a little that time to keep warm. You could have hot steel on and be stopped by the snow—and I've seen a ladle of steel freeze over, get hard—a solid chunk. They'd have to burn that out in sections with acetylene, turn it out of the ladle and put it in the furnace again. Sit on the train so long it would cool right down.

But you know—I liked it. I got used to it and I liked it. I was there 49 years on the one job. Money wasn't the thing at all. I started to work there for 14 cents an hour—General Yard, labourer. But when I went brakeman, I got a cent more. You had to work seven days to make eight dollars a week. Very little money.

I was pensioned off in 1958, and the only time I ever put money into the bank was after I quit work.

Jimmy Hines: A View from the Open Hearth

JIMMY HINES: I started in the Steel Plant in 1922. I was 15 years of age—just a week before school opened. I left school in the eighth grade and I never went back. My father was in the plant before me—he ran a cold saw. In those days, they rolled a rail and put it out on a cooling bed. They'd be different lengths, and they would have to be cut cold to a certain length. He was operating this great big circular saw. There were no teeth in it—just little gouges about the size of the tip of your finger, into a big blade. And this would be going like the hobs of hell. He'd set the rail the proper length, and then he'd come down with this saw. That was his job till he finished up.

I started in the Open Hearth office, keeping records of other fellows working. And I said to myself, To hell with that, let *them* keep records of what *I* do. And I went into the mill.

And in those days everything was by hand—that is, into the furnace, the Open Hearth. I went in there as Third Helper. There was a Melter and a Second Help-er—three of us at the Open Hearth. When that furnace was tapped and we'd make the bottom, the crew from another furnace—the Second and Third Helper—would come down and help us make up the bottom. Otherwise, there was just three of a crew.

The Open Hearth furnace starts off empty after tapping out. We'd prepare that furnace to be charged up again. We'd have to fill

71

it in to the slag line. And it would be hot, you know. You had just tapped out a heat, and you have to keep heat there sufficient to melt down the steel. And in those days it was heated by the old gas producers, operated by men shovelling coal out of a great big hopper into a fire down below, burning coal in a silo, like. The gas off that would come down through a sort of tunnel, across the floor, and right into the Open Hearth furnace. It would go through what they call a checker.

Say we had the gases coming in on the north end, right through the furnace and out on the south end. The reason for that is that the gas going out the checkers [a great big tunnel affair checkered with bricks crossways, with holes between]—those bricks would have to get heated up. So that when the cold air would be coming in, when it reverses, that checker would be

Pouring a test

good and hot, and the cold air coming in with the gases would heat up as well before it gets to the furnace.

The gas would come through the checkers and right up into the furnace. Automatically burn when it'd come in. It would be coming in as a flame. When it hit the checkers it would sharpen up that flame. And when it hit the furnace it would be bang, bang, bang. Burning all the time. Until the furnace was tapped out. Then the producers would ease up on it. There would be a gas producer for each furnace, and all those men would be doing would be shovelling coal.

The Blast Furnace made the iron. The Open Hearth is changing the iron into steel by mixing it with a certain quantity of limestone, iron ore, and scrap steel. You put the limestone in first. At that time it was around 10 or 12 boxes. That would be charged into the furnace with what they called the charging car. Then they charge the ore, an amount according to the kind of heat you were charging for. If you were charging for a rail, you wouldn't put as much ore in as you would for soft steel, a low-carbon heat. Because if you charge too much ore, the heat would come soft and be metallurgically no good for rails, the carbon would be too low. Four-carbon steel— that would be riveting. Right up to a rail, which would be 69 to 70 carbon—quite a difference in the ore you'd charge.

Teeming a ladle of steel into ingot molds.
Then (opposite, right) the glowing ingots, after the molds have been stripped.

The foreman would tell you "Charge back for a rail" or "Charge back for a soft"—and the carbon you were making—and that would be your next job. If I was told to charge a soft heat, an ordinary soft heat—that'd be 18 to 23 carbon—I'd have to find out how the silicon in the iron was running. And if that's running normally around 90 or 100 silicon, I have to charge an amount of ore to take care of that.

Say if I was charging for a soft heat, I'd charge it with eight or nine boxes of ore; but if I was charging for a rail heat, a higher carbon, I would cut down on the charging ore, charge about four or five boxes of ore. When the molten iron goes in, it starts boiling them. Then as we go along and I break a test—what I mean by breaking a test, you pour a bit of metal in a little iron box and it solidifies, and the Third Helper would knock it out and cool it off in a water pan. He'd bring it to me when I was the First Helper, and I would have to turn around and judge the carbon—judge it according to the grain of the fracture.

(*Now, do they call one of the managers in to make this deci-*

sion?) No, no. No way. (*It's important for me to know that. Who was making the decisions on the floor, in the Steel Plant?*) The foreman's job is, when I get the heat ready, he's to come down and tap it out. That's his job. That's it and it only. He'll turn around and say, "Your next one will be for a soft heat"—or whatever—carbon, and he'd be gone and you wouldn't see him anymore till the next heat you'd be ready to tap.

Everything depended on the men on the furnace. It was in their hands. The foreman doesn't come down and take over the furnace and tell me what to do or anything. If there's, say, a green helper and he's not too sure of himself, he might rather go to an old hand on the next furnace than go to the foreman. (*How would the old hand treat him?*) Oh, good. Same as his buddy.

(*Were there classes?*) No, no, no, no. There was one class over there—steelworker—and that was it. (*I mean, did they ever take the helpers and set them in a classroom and teach them how to judge that test break?*) No way. You taught yourself. For instance, I started as Third Helper, and it was my job to break those tests, and I'd have to take them to the First Helper, the Melter—he'd judge the carbon according to the grain and I'd ask him questions. That's where *I* learned. And when I was Melter, if I thought it was high, I'd have to use more ore to get the carbon down.

People may have forgotten, but we really had steelworkers here. When I worked there, men were proud to work there, and they

took pride in their work, I'll tell you that. And they had skilled steelworkers, the best—and I'm saying that not primarily to put myself up there, because there were men over there better than me. I had to learn from those fellows. They were just going around doing their ordinary jobs, running the furnace, and I'd just watch what they were doing, and that's how I'd learn. It's the men on that furnace—that's who's making that steel.

The procedure I'm telling you about is back in the old dark days of making steel—nearly all by hand. Previous to that, when the first Open Hearth furnace started, *everything*, everything was put in by hand. But not here. When this mill started, it was at the stage of mechanical loaders to charge the furnace. The charging car operator would be running this machine on rails. It had a ram on it, 14 or 15 feet long. It would pick up the box on a car in front of the furnace, pick it up with a ram, go right into the furnace through the door, and electrically turn the pan over and dump it. The Melter would tell that charging car operator how much stone to put in, how much ore to put in—and scrap would be there, of course. Scrap steel. General scrap. Pieces of pipe, ends cut off of the rails, the ends of the blooms in the Blooming Mill come back to the Open Hearth to be re-melted—and carloads of scrap coming into the plant all the time. Charging car was all electrically operated. But there's nothing electric as far as those of us at the furnace working a heat. We did it damn well the hard way and sweated it out. It was all done by hand. The men working the gas producers—all hand work. And those of us at the furnace, different materials going in, all by hand.

When the furnace was charging, the Second Helper and I would be over at the back of the furnace, cleaning out the runner. The runner would be a long spout at the back of the furnace from the tap hole. Finished metal would come out the tap hole along this runner and into a ladle. And we'd have to clean that old scrap off and re-mud it so that next time we tap out, the metal coming out will run on this mud. Just an ordinary clay we'd plaster with a trowel. Then the next heat, when you'd finish the tapping out, it'll be easy again to get the scrap off the runner.

Then by the time you'd get that work finished, the furnace would be finished charging and we'd have to go over to the front.

And after all this process of working the heat, making the bottom and charging the furnace, the tracks in front of the furnace would be dirty—and it would be up to the Second and Third Helpers to clean up the tracks. Then following that, it would be just about the proper time to sit down and make tea and have lunch. And while we were having our lunch, the First Helper would be ordering the metal—that would be iron from the Blast Furnace. It would be brought up and stored in what they called the mixer. The iron would be stored in there as a hot liquid for whenever any of the Open Hearth furnaces would want it. And the helpers' job was to hook up the ladle to the charging car, which had a great big cable with a big hook on it coming down—hook up the metal ladle and poured that metal into the furnace. It would generally take about three ladles. And of course the Melter would be standing over by the wall, taking it all in, doing nothing.

Then we wouldn't be doing anything until the scrap in the furnace would be melted down and the limestone would be coming up, except that we were reversing the furnace—the gas and air through the checkers, every 15 minutes—and that was by hand. And in the meantime the First Helper, the Melter, would be taking stock of the furnace, taking charge of it. And once the limestone started coming up he'd say, "Okay, boys, we'll give her the spar [fluorspar]." Now, he'd pull the door up. Great big chains coming down controlled it. We'd have to give him a hand sometimes, pulling the door up—then we'd get into the spar bin and shovel spar in.

There were three doors in the old furnaces. And it wasn't just a matter of throwing it in the door—you'd have to spread it around like on the farm, all over that stone. And you can imagine that heat, with the furnace door up, and you're looking into a path of melted steel, and the flame on the furnace all the time. And you're in front of it. Damn well right it's hot. The months of July and August, it was damn hot. Well I'll tell you! And the floor from the furnace over to the front of the mill—it would be so hot in the summertime you could fry eggs on it. Heavy boots and heavy soles. Because the checkers from the gas producers were underneath that floor—and we were getting all the heat. And wintertime wasn't so bad, but you'd be sweating in front of the furnace, and then when the heat was over, you'd have to get in a shack somewhere where there's some heat to keep warm. Or bundle up close to the furnace.

Now you're past the spar stage and it's time to pour a test. If it was coming in high carbon, it was the job of the Second and Third Helpers to get into the ore again. Well, I've seen us there, working long hours on Sunday night. Now every second Sunday, we'd have to work a long shift—24 hours. If you worked the long shift, you could schedule a night off to the week. So this Sunday I started in, working a heat, and we got to the test stage and had to shovel ore— heat was coming in high. Well, we shoveled four boxes of ore, which would amount to close to 10 tons. In the middle of July. I said to the fellow working with me, "After a day like this I'm not coming out again tonight. I'm not risking going through another thing like this in one day." "Oh, come on out," he said, "I'll charge the ore"—which meant, the more ore that's charged, the less we'd probably have to shovel by hand. If the test came in any ways close. Whether he did or not, I don't know to this day. He said he had the ore charged. And he got a dose of high-silica iron. After supper I came back, started in the whole process—and after the test, we had to shovel four more boxes of ore, about another 10 tons. And I got home that morning and my mother said, "Get rid of that job. Don't go back."

But I liked it. I liked the work. (*Liked it? It was hot....*) Yes, went through hell. But it was interesting to me. And I really loved it.

Anyhow, you continue on putting in the ore until you get the carbon down to where you think it's ready—then you send the test into the lab. Say you were making 18 to 23 carbon—ordinary soft steel—you could make anything with it—nails, wire, rods—you get her down to about 20 carbon, you're ready to tap out.

And when the foreman'd tap it, it would all go out into this great big ladle, which would be dropped underneath the spout of the furnace by an overhead crane—a ladle holding 50 ton of steel— you can imagine the size. Pour that metal, and the crane would pick it up and carry it over to the molds. And they'd fill those molds as long as the metal was there to fill them. And then a little narrow-gauge engine would come down and hook up on that string of molds with metal in them and take them up to the mills for rolling. End up in the hands of a guy like Wally Chandler in the Rolling Mill.

From the time it leaves the Open Hearth, it goes to the Blooming Mill first. Those ingots would be cold by the time they got up there. They would have to be put in what they call the soaking pits, to re-heat the ingots up to the proper temperature before they could roll them. A big crane would drop tongs down, like ice tongs, and bring them up and lay them on the rolling grid in the Blooming Mill. They would roll that big ingot down to what they call a bloom. That would be about 10 inch square and three or four times the length of the ingot. And that bloom, it would go through another mill—the Billet Mill—which would roll it down smaller, and yes, about three times the length of the bloom. And then it would go from there to the Rod and Bar Mill. This is soft steel, now. Remember that. This is not the steel that would become rails. Soft steel is made into wire for nails or wire itself or rods and bars for reinforcing concrete.

(*Now if it had been high carbon steel, the harder steel....*) It'd be a bloom in the Blooming Mill, rolling it from an ingot to a bloom, for rails. And that bloom will go down to the Rail Mill. It will come in here as a square bloom and go through another set of rollers. They keep rolling it back and forth—red hot—until it gets shaped into a rail.

Wally Chandler: Catching Steel

WALLY CHANDLER: I went into the Steel Plant in May 1925. My father was in the mill before me. He started in 1905. He was a sailor man before that. And a farmer in Prince Edward Island. In 1946 he was pensioned off at 74 years of age. Oh, he was a powerful man—6 foot 1, weighed 210 pounds, and his wrists were half again as big as mine. No fat of any kind. In the Steel Plant he was catching steel. My father worked from the meager jobs in the Rod Mill up to finishing, which was next to top man. But then he left that mill and came over into the Bar Mill, catching steel. Catching it with tongs.

The bar would come out. You'd grab it, swing it around with those big long steel tongs in your hands. (*Would the bar be hot?*) I should say. And this was what our type of work was—catching all the time, day in and day out, hour after hour, coming as fast as ever it could spew it out. This was our job.

In those days we rolled all sizes from one-quarter-inch round and one-quarter-inch square to all sizes of round and square. All sizes of round up to two-inch round. Now you can imagine a 32nd and a 64th—these were sizes. We rolled 500 different sizes in my day in the mill, different sizes in rounds, flats, squares, truss bars, angles—and now they only roll high bond, for concrete, with the knobs on it. They only roll nine sections. And we rolled 500. All the commercial bars are gone.

When I first went to work, I went with my father. If I had been in the Bar Mill three more months, I would have had 48 years in the Bar Mill alone. I was almost 17 when I went on. I went into the General Yard for three months, part-time work—just anything that came up, that they'd need men. We didn't get brass checks at that time; we got cardboard, because we were only temporary.

And there were three men on the mill all the time—catching. They'd work 15 minutes and they'd come off, three more men would go on. Half-time job. You only spent half time. Sometimes you could stay half an hour. Then the other man had a half hour off. It was that strenuous you'd usually work 15 minutes. If it got a little smaller and not so hot, you could work half an hour.

All the time I was working on the lesser jobs, I was going up there, catching, breaking in. I'd get the last one at dinnertime. If I missed it, well, go down and wind it up. If the regular catcher missed it, it went to the scrap machine and you had to bail it up—they had a man there to do that. But the last one at dinnertime, if I missed that, I had to go down and wind it up. And I didn't miss any. I could get ahold of it all right. And then I got the last one at the end of the day. That wouldn't interfere with anybody. They're all gone to dinner and they're all going home.

And that's the way I broke in.

When I got catching, I was only on it for 10 years, and this was as a spar catcher for most of those years. We had a six-catcher mill. They didn't need me on the seventh. When they came to an eight-catcher mill, I would go on, with another one. I would only be on the mill when there'd be seven or eight—and this would be occasionally. But then, when the mill went from one shift of 10 hours a day to two shifts of 10 hours a day, then I got promoted. I was on catching continuously for about seven years. Then she went three shifts [eight hours each]. But in the meantime, I had been promoted from catching to roughing. Where I used to be in charge of two pair of rollers, now I was in charge of six pair of rollers, with three helpers. I was responsible for setting those rollers up and getting the stuff out in its proper shape. She goes straight line in the sixth. But when it comes to the seventh roller, the catcher grabs it, turns around and puts it in 8, and it whisks around to 9. He'll catch it, stick it in 10; it'll go around to 11. And he puts it into

Catching steel in the Rod Mill. The white smoking line is hot steel. It is getting thinner as it is caught and turned back and passed through the rollers.

12, which is the last one—and that's the finished product. And each one of these rollers is gradually reducing it to size. And there is a man there who is a finisher—this was finally my job—and the way finishing works is this: the roller will send the right amount of stock from the first roll to the 11th, so that I can manipulate it so that the finished product will be just what the customer wants within seven thousandths. I have a stick. As the finished bar comes by, I put the stick down one side and it burns an impression on the stick. Then I get another impression burned on the other side. I read those impressions—whether there is enough thickness on that bar or too much. And I can adjust that before it gets into the 11th stand. If I've got too much, I've got to reduce it by closing the 11th. And I've got to be right there because she's coming, boy, just like that, one after another, I suppose 35 miles an hour. And they're only coming a little bit apart. They're coming around nearly end to end.

Sometimes it's so close that the catcher is confused, that he grabs the last end of the one ahead. So he's pretty cagey. When it's coming around, it's in the dark and he can't see it coming. But when it comes out of number 10, that's when we'll say there's a few inches he can see. Now, when he sees the reflection—not the bar—'cause when it's coming around it casts a reflection ahead of it—and when he sees that reflection, he says to himself, like I've said many times: "One, two," and catch. You don't say "three" because she's gone. You're catching with nothing there—just the length for you to whip it into the next one.

And the heat is terrific—120 degrees in there, saturated with pollution and dust. Smoke. Oh my god, perspiring. Not as a finisher, but as a catcher. As a finisher I'm just standing there burning wood all day. But I'm making the final adjustments, and when it goes by me, it's good or bad. And there's inspectors up there accepting it or rejecting it. If he gets too many rejected he comes down, something wrong, getting too much scrap. And that rejection is thrown off the bed and they chop it up and put it in scrap pans and ship it back to Mr. Hines there, and they make it all over again.

But we've rolled many, many days without one rejection. We've rolled a thousand billets a day and we wouldn't lose one. It's remarkable. I did this in the days when it was 10 hours in the Bar Mill, and in the Rod Mill they were working 11 and 13. And when I was catching, it was usually 15 minutes on, 15 off. You could play cards or have something to eat, or you could walk out in the yard and get the cool air. But it was an occupation that kept you on edge. The least thing would set you off. And we used to get paid basic rate plus tonnage. Now if you were rolling the small section, you'd have to roll quite a bit to accumulate any amount of tonnage. But rolling the heavy stuff, your tonnage would go up quite fast. But in so doing—my God, man, you're working like a bloody mule.

But we were young those days. I've seen it when it was only fun. We were standing there screaming, "Get 'em out, get 'em out!"

But if I had it to do over again, that'd be the last place I'd go to. Us fellows, we were dropouts from school—we didn't want to go to school, we wanted to go to work, get money, and wanted to have some fun. But now that we know better, if we had our day over, I think we would go to school.

Bernie Gallaway:
"There are two kinds of men...."

BERNIE GALLAWAY: I used to get a newspaper from the West. A fellow came down, trying to organize the steelworkers, used to have meetings over in Wentworth Park. He started, but never got anywhere. One Big Union. The idea was to have every working man in one union. That started in Winnipeg in around 1919. J. S.

Woodsworth started that. That's what the superintendent in the Coke Oven department used to call me, "O.B.U." "Where's that O.B.U. today?" I had hope for that, yes.

I was a miner before I was a steelworker, and I'd get a slip about that length—about a foot or more—pay slips. And at one end you might have made $30 if you were in contract, 25 or 30. Then when you'd read along and get to the other end of the slip, after all the deductions—probably you'd have 50 cents. And in the Steel Plant [after 1923], the lowest rates, used to bring home $19 a week.

And *then* the Depression. Earned an average of nine bucks a week through it. I fared off fairly well because I used to get one shift a week, one day's work. Used to get that and five dollars a week relief from the city—a great help.

I'll give you an idea how it was. One day I went out and the boss told us to stay around. So anyway, he gave me and another man a job on Sunday—on Sunday—unloading a car of lime. That's some nice job. Taking it out of a car with a shovel. And it went up your nose and in your mouth and you're burning up—and you're all in for a week after you unload a car of lime with a shovel. Your nose bleeding and everything. And a young fellow came along and he started talking to us—we were in the car, shovelling—"My heavens," he said, "you fellows are lucky." My buddy said, "You get away before I cut your head off with a shovel, calling us lucky." And then I'm on my way home, up Victoria Road, there was a bootlegging joint there, and three or four men out on the verandah talking. One fellow says, "That bugger there's lucky. He's working."

I worked in the Coke Ovens department, where you produce coke, and at that time they used to produce ammonia salt in the by-product plant. It was part of the Coke Oven department. They gave that up in later years. Coke was 95 per cent of the Coke Oven department. I worked at producing the ammonia salt—that's a ferti-lizer. And you needed sulfuric acid for that. And they had a sulfuric acid plant, and I worked in the sulfuric acid plant for 39 years, making the acid. They'd sell that ammonia salt to farmers—mostly to China one time. And in the acid plant where I worked, we didn't go the full year. You drove for 10 months. Then you'd have to close her down because the acid is hard on the lead—you had to stop for repairs. The vats—chambers 50 feet by 50 feet and 75 feet high. Then there were smaller ones. An awful lot of lead used. We closed down anyway for about two months. And we'd go out in the yard to work. Then the plant closed down altogether in 1962. The company claimed they lost the market for ammonia salt. They tore down the building and the acid plant.

When I retired I was getting $2.75 an hour. Thirty-three cents when I went there. Retired in 1964. After working 39 years.

And I'll tell you the worst of it. I went over to town to a doctor to examine me for insurance. I haven't seen the poor old fellow since. And when he examined me he said, "Where did you work?" I said, "I worked in the Coke Ovens, in an acid plant." "How many years you work there?" he asked. I told him. "My God," he said, "you're supposed to be dead."

There are two kinds of men, like I told you before. There's always a bunch of men that are satisfied, they never want anything—they work when the men are out on strike—they go along and do their work and do what they're told, and they don't want any unions. Or

anything. Then you'll find the other kind of fellow is active, and he's interested in unions. He wants to make himself better and his people better...and he gets interested in politics and everything that affects your life. But others you'll find are just "Come day, go day, God sends Sunday"—they used to say.

(*Would you say you were radical?*) Well, I wanted things changed from what I was getting. I would fight. Some said I was communist, but I didn't know then what communist is. If I knew what it is, probably I was it. But I read a lot about it and I heard a lot about it. From the time I was a kid of nine years old, you couldn't put a piece of paper up in a post office in my home town but I had to read it. Sometimes I picked books up off the street and took them home and read them.

You'll find a fellow who's satisfied, and he's going to tell you a story that on the wages he was getting he got along all right, and he didn't mind it. And you'll get another man, and he'll tell you he went through hell, we should have been doing this, we should have got that—we're humans and we're supposed to get as much as anybody else who's trying to get a good living in this world. He's active, you see. He wants something.

I was on the Grievance Committee, fighting for the men. And the credit union—I got interested in that. And the cooperative store. I don't believe in capitalism. I claim that capitalism is no good and it's got to change some day. But what it's going to change to, I don't know.

CHAPTER 4

The 1923 Steel Strike
and Coal Miners' Sympathy Strike

THE ORDER OF EVENTS:

On June 28, 1923, steelworkers at Sydney went out on strike against the British Empire Steel Corporation (BESCO). Within hours, federal troops were called up to aid local civil power, "in anticipation of disorders that might arise." And from Halifax, a provincial police force was sent to Sydney. The first detachment of federal troops arrived early on the morning of Saturday, June 30. The provincial police, with the troops to back them up, entered into direct engagement with strikers and bystanders, resulting the next day (July 1) in "Bloody Sunday." With that, J. B. McLachlan brought out the District 26 miners in a 100 per cent strike. Eventually, the miners closed not only Cape Breton and mainland mines, but District 18 in Alberta came out as well in support of the steelworkers—all demanding the recall of the troops and provincial police.

Views from the Steel Plant

J. B. McLachlan and Dan Livingstone were arrested, originally for publishing what the *Sydney Post* called "a false picture" of the events of Bloody Sunday. McLachlan was eventually tried for seditious libel and sentenced to two years in Dorchester Penitentiary, of which about four months were served. John L. Lewis, the American leader of the United Mine Workers International, demanded the miners return to work. When they refused, he revoked the District 26 charter, removed the radical executive, put in his own slate of officers, and sent the miners back to work. Without the coal miners' support, the steelworkers' strike was doomed—but they did hold on for a while. Finally, faced with a combination of forces against them—legislation banning groups larger than three people (which effectively destroyed picketing), starvation, jail sentences, the Steel Plant's resumption of operations, and the announcement that strikers must vacate the corporation's housing—the steelworkers resolved to go back to work.

What follows is not only a story of the events of 1923 as told by people who were there—Doane Curtis, Dan MacKay, Mr. and Mrs. Bernie Gallaway, and Emerson Campbell. It is also the story of how those events were reported by the newspapers of the time. The two principle newspapers used here are the *Sydney Post* and the *Maritime Labour Herald*. Neither newspaper can be said to give us a balanced, accurate account. They do, however, clearly preserve the bias and tone of the time.

DAN MACKAY: I think we should say a word about why we had to organize. The reason we organized was the intolerable conditions that we were labouring under on that plant at that time. The hours were 11 hours by day, 13 hours by night, seven days a week, no holidays, no vacations. In fact it was a common saying then that the steelworker going home, particularly in the wintertime, never saw his family until the next spring—because he went to work and they were in bed and they were in bed when he came home. We were slaving under conditions that were hard in this day and age for anyone to believe. You were at the whim and wish of the boss. The boss could send you home. If he didn't like the colour of your hair, if he didn't like the church you went to, if he didn't like the way you voted on election day—he could send you home and there were no questions asked.

The men themselves decided there had to be something done. And the union was organized and slowly worked up to the 1923 strike. It was one of savagery by all governments in power at that time. They sent their soldiers down here. The provincial police galloped up and down the streets of our city, they trampled our women and children, they had no regard for anyone. The 1923 strike is history that I hope will never be repeated in the island of Cape Breton.

EMERSON CAMPBELL: I was born on September 2, 1887. The first work I did was labouring around when they were still building the Steel Plant. I remember when it was just barren ground there. My first job was pick and shovel, 15 cents an hour, 10 hours a day—no holidays, no nothing. I was down in the Rail Mill the day the first rail came through. I think that was about 1906. I got more money when I went straightening rails.

But I wasn't on that plant a month when I saw there was something wrong, and I was only from the country. I didn't know a steel bar from a log. I said there is something wrong working those long hours and all that sort of stuff. And I started talking about a union.

I'll give you an example. In the Rail Mill I was getting three dollars and a half a day, which was big money. And my helper—he

89

was a coloured chap—he was getting 15 cents an hour—and I couldn't make a dollar without him, without his help. And another thing, when you had a grievance, you'd go and try to settle it. If you went to the boss and he said, "No, no, that's it, the guy's no good, he was drunk yesterday and drunk the day before"—that was it. That was as far as you could go without a union. And they wouldn't pay the same. The way I figured it, if you were a good fellow with the boss, well he'd give you a few more cents an hour. It wasn't a man's ability at all—just being a good fellow. And in those days there was no compensation. The government nor the company never looked after the men in any way.

So I saw there was something wrong and I kept on and kept on and got some more with me and we got started. I was part of the executive when the strike was on. Jack MacIntyre, he was president. Forman Waye was secretary. I was vice-president. I joined the union right at the beginning—the Amalgamated Association of Iron, Steel, and Tin Workers.

ROY WOLVIN, *head of BESCO*, June 22, 1923: "The policy of the Dominion Iron and Steel Company is to maintain the open shop.... Trade unionism is wrong in principle...and will not be tolerated by the company."

Maritime Labour Herald, June 28, 1923:
...The Steelworkers' Union has declared a strike to enforce better conditions for the steelworkers...in the hell called the Steel Plant at Sydney. The wages range from 30 cents an hour for the lowest paid workers to 57 cents an hour for machinists. Every week-end a twenty-four hour shift is worked. Out of the 3800 men employed at the plant 65 per cent of them are paid the grand sum of 32 cents an hour.

The strike came suddenly after negotiations had been carried on with the British Empire Steel Corporation since last March. D. H. McDougall and his gang were quite willing to chat pleasantly with the steelworkers from the plant, but they would not recognize the union, nor would they grant the demands of the workers. These demands are: A 20 per cent increase in wages and a check-off for the collection of the union dues. The carefully laid plans of the union worked without a hitch. At 3 a.m. Thursday morning the night shift moved off the plant and picketed the gates and were joined by the day shift as they came to work. From chatting with the steelworkers, D. H. McDougall and his gang of labour skinners must now turn to working if they want to keep the plant running.

The management tried desperately to split the union by starting a "company union" on Wednesday. They sang the old song of the exploiters of labour in Cape Breton: "Your leaders are too 'red,' break away from them and we will look after you." This siren song failed to win a single worker from the union. The union ranks are solid and will remain so despite the fairy tales of the management and the spies and pimps that they have planted in the union. The steelworkers know the enemy they are fighting. They know that Armstrong [Premier of Nova Scotia] and his government will try to send provincial police to Sydney to "preserve law and order." They know that BESCO will use force if they are sure the workers will not destroy the plant in retaliation. But if BESCO tries any of these stunts the big brother of the Steelworkers' Union of Sydney, the miners of Cape Breton, will take a hand in the struggle.

Sydney Post:
RIOTING AND RAIDING STRIKERS ATTACK AND DEFY POLICE
The policy of "peaceful picketing" enunciated by Pres. McIntyre of the Steelworkers' union, at the commencement of the strike at Besco plant yesterday [June 28], went by the board late in the evening, when a gang of men entered the works by way of the Coke Ovens, which is located outside the high board fence that surrounds the other section of the plant.

It is estimated that about a hundred strikers, the majority of them young men, made their way into the works through the ward five area, and to the accompaniment of a medley of hurrahs and other mob noises, rushed No. One boiler house, from which they drove the maintenance men who were keeping the fires going in the furnaces at that place.

Their object was, apparently, to frighten the men who failed to heed the strike order and quit work. As far as *The Post* could learn at a late hour last night they were unsuccessful in this respect, as the only ones to leave were those forcefully driven off....

When the strikers congregated at the Coke Ovens, evidently bent on mischief, a hurry up call was sent to the city for assistance. Chief McCormick and his deputy, accompanied by the sheriffs Ingraham, Magistrate Hill and a squad of police, went to the plant.

Surrounded by city and steel company officers Mr. Hill started to read the Riot Act to the mob, when he was assailed by a shower of missiles from a dozen different directions, one of which hit him on the head, knocking him unconscious. He was taken to No. 4 gate house where he recovered and was later taken to his home. No material damage was caused to any section of the plant during the outbreak.

All activity centred on Victoria Road in the vicinity of No. 4 gate, where thousands of men gathered early in the evening prepared for a demonstration. The city police were summoned and on their arrival with the police patrol wagon they were greeted with a fusilade of stones. Despite the valiant efforts of the handful of city and company police, who attempted to oppose the mob with their batons, the gate was rushed and men who were working were dragged forth to be paraded up and down Victoria Road amid the jeers of the mob.

EMERSON CAMPBELL: The strikers were told what to do, they'd get instructions, and they would do it. We had no trouble. (*The* Post *reports they were trying to tear down the fence to get into the Steel Plant, that they wanted to stop the men manning the boilers.*) I don't know about them actually tearing down the fence, but they wanted to get to the men inside. But I would say they would have wanted some of the men on the boilers to *stay* on the boilers. If they all came out the Blast Furnace was out. That Blast Furnace would be at least two months before it could be lit up again, and probably have an explosion. So the strikers did not want the boilers to be turned off.

As far as I'm concerned the *Post* made a terrible lot of mistakes. Probably I make mistakes too. One man's opinion, I say no. The steelworkers were not trying to destroy the plant. After all, that would be their bread and butter. What in the hell were they going to do? They had to work there when it was over. There was, what, 2800 steelworkers in that strike.

But you must remember this: it was all new to the steelworkers, new to all of us. New to me. New to the executive. Anything

Federal troops—Royal Canadian Dragoons—encamped
at the Sydney Steel Plant, July 1923

went wrong, well, what will we do? What will we do? The executive would always get the steelworkers' opinion, the rank and file. What will we do? That way we had the backing of the steelworkers, and we knew at all times pretty well where we were.

GEORGE MACEACHERN: But of course there was violence. You couldn't go on a peaceful strike with no money in your pocket. So many people stayed in [the plant] that it was next to impossible. The steelworkers had to fight and fight they did.

Sydney Post:
SEVERAL RAIDS ON STEEL PLANT ATTEMPTED BY STRIKERS
      The police guarding the Steel Plant had another stiff time last night [June 29] with a mob of strikers at No. 4 gate. Several raids on the plant were attempted by the strikers who numbered over a thousand, but the

force of officers were successful in holding the men off and preventing them from wreaking damage on the plant, which was apparently their purpose. During the night a number of the police suffered minor injuries by blows from rocks thrown in the dark in the direction of the gate house. The casualties among the strikers were more numerous. Not a few of the men were quite severely clubbed.

Things were fairly quiet about No. 4 gate all afternoon. About six o'clock the strikers began to gather and by eight o'clock a thousand or fifteen hundred of them were crowded in the street outside the fence. On the outside of the fence Chief McCormick and a half dozen of his men took up patrol. A force of steel and coal company police numbering about a dozen were stationed inside the entrance.

At nine o'clock the stage was set for something to happen. The men were in a belligerent mood as was evidenced by the hoots and jeers they hurled at the police. The leaders among the strikers were doing their best to work their fellows into fighting spirit and in this they were fairly successful.

Things began to look nasty about nine o'clock. "Let us inside, boys," some of the strikers started yelling. The shout was taken up by hundreds of the men and a shower of rocks followed. The police took whatever shelter they could find about the gate to protect themselves from the missiles which flew towards them in the dark. The stoning continued for several minutes. Large rocks bounced from the roof and walls of the gate house and the electric lights about the entrance were smashed.

The fusilade of rocks ended suddenly and the strikers, thinking that the barrage on the police had made matters simple, rushed the entrance. As many as could catch hold of the gate fastened on and pushed it open. A dozen policemen sprang side by side into the breach and with sticks ready for action succeeded in holding the strikers off. When the crowd backed up the officers closed the entrance.

Now, worked to a high pitch of excitement, some of the strikers decided that to tear the fence down would be a simpler way of getting into the works. One man started to cut a hole into the fence with an axe. Others went to a point a hundred yards north of the gate and tore boards away, making a hole big enough for a dozen men to enter at a time. The more daring of the mob went through the hole and stopping there encouraged their comrades with loud shouts to follow them....

94

The 1923 Steel Strike

Royal Canadian Horse Artillery at Sydney

In a few minutes a crowd of about a hundred men gathered inside the fence and started towards the gate to take the police officers at the rear. Wildly yelling and waving clubs in the air they marched along inside the fence. Ten feet away from the gate the mob stopped short. The men in the front ranks brandished their weapons in the faces of the police and demanded that the gate be opened.

"We'll open it if you want to go outside," one officer shouted at them. Without waiting for an answer the police swung the gate open. A few of the strikers on the street joined their fellows inside and ignoring the police they started through the plant to the boiler house which seemed to be the one object of their attentions. At the boiler house they got a reception which made them wish they had never entered the plant....

About four hundred faithful employees of the company who remained on the jobs when the strike was called, were organized into a defensive force by Capt. D. A. Noble.... While the mob outside howled and rushed the gates, this force of men remained drawn up in readiness near the boiler house, the main objective of the strikers, to repel any attack which the vandals outside the fence might make. Armed with iron bars and each man with a white cloth band about his arm as a mark of identification, they made a formidable looking force. When the party of one hundred men who forced their way through a gap in the fence, approached the boiler house with the intention of driving out the men who operated it, they met this force of employees and got the surprise of their lives. The police and the defence men attacked the raiders and put them to flight in less time than it takes to tell it.

Union leaders who have made the statement that less than a hundred steelworkers remain on the plant should have viewed this force of

Views from the Steel Plant

Royal Canadian Regiment encampment at Number 1 Gate, BESCO, 1923

defensive men on Friday to find out their mistake. They numbered about three hundred and they were as anxious to protect the plant from damage as any policeman. This defensive force is made up of only a part of the men still remaining on the plant. As many more are engaged in maintenance work about the various mills.

Sydney Post:
SOLDIERS WILL PROTECT STEEL PLANT
FROM FURTHER DAMAGE
With two hundred and fifty trained infantry and artillerymen to hold off the attacks of the mobs who have been conducting raids on the Steel Plant since the steelworkers' strike started, the officials of the company anticipate no further trouble. There is a general feeling of relief in the city this morning over the arrival of the troops [June 30].... [Strikers] were not in a fighting mood. They stood quietly and watched the soldiers on picket duty about the entrance. Military pickets are distributed about all of the strategic points on the edges of the plant this morning.... The force is made up of small drafts from the various units of Halifax, Royal Canadian Garrison Artillery, Royal Canadian Horse Artillery, Royal Canadian Regiment and Army Service Corps....
ENTERED IN WARLIKE STYLE
The troops arrived shortly after four o'clock and they made their entrance into the city somewhat along the war-like lines adopted by the

military during the recent strike of coal miners. Before the train an armoured gondola was pushed. The sides were piled high with sand bags and [the] car bristled with machine guns. A light engine [preceded] the troop train over the railway spur into the Steel Plant to make sure that no damage had been done to the track by the strikers. A force of constables patrolled the track all evening to prevent any happening of the kind but every precaution against damage to the train was nevertheless taken.

HON. JAMES MURDOCK, *federal Minister of Labour*: "It is the popular impression...that the Dominion government sent the troops to Sydney. Under the militia act, commanding officers of military districts are bound to furnish protection in areas where the local civil authorities call upon them to do so. That is what happened in Sydney. The first troops were sent from Halifax in response to the order of the Sydney authorities before the federal government knew anything about the matter."

TOM MOORE, *President of the Trades and Labour Congress of Canada*: "Military forces were rushed to the scene and upon the requisition of one man (Judge Finlayson of Sydney) and not on the request of the municipal authorities, who should be the best informed as to any possible danger existing or likely to exist against public safety."

PRIME MINISTER MACKENZIE KING: "Perhaps I should say that some days ago I took steps to make it known to His Honour Judge Finlayson, to the officer commanding the district and the Premier of Nova Scotia, that our government viewed with some concern the numbers of troops which had been requisitioned in aid of the civil power in Cape Breton, and made it quite clear that we were most anxious that the military forces should be withdrawn just as rapidly as circumstances would permit."

Added to this—wrote the *Post*—Mr. Murdock, Minister of Labour, "informs an astonished people he has not the slightest doubt but that the forwarding of the troops to Cape Breton was to say the least premature, and he would do everything in his power to have the soldiers removed with all possible despatch."

EMERSON CAMPBELL: And the provincial police came down from

Views from the Steel Plant

Halifax. They were drunk all the time. They had 15 horses when they left Halifax and they put them in the boxcar and when they got in Sydney they were all dead. Smothered. Then they had to go and get some of the coal-haulers' horses here. But they were drunk

all the time they were here. I guess to get the job you had to be a drunk. They had batons about four feet long, made right here in the Steel Plant. Strapped on their wrists just like a wrist watch. And they were swinging them. Good hardwood in them. They were made right down here in the plant in the carpenter shop. I knew a fellow right down here was making them. He didn't know what the hell he was making or who he was making them for.

DOANE CURTIS: After they took over coal-haulers' horses, the first raid the provincial police made was on the city warehouse where they kept the stuff to cheer us. And after that they went up to the city hall and were told by Colonel MacDonald he was going to "put on a show" that evening. [That the strikers were to be deliberately "aggravated," and that MacDonald was then going to have the provincial police "put on a show" was sworn to before a Royal Commission by a sergeant of the Sydney city police force.]

They galloped down to Whitney Pier, past 4 Gate and on the main street of Whitney Pier with their gallant army and their well-lit army, because that's what they were. With four-foot batons. And they went up and down the street hitting people on the sidewalk. Some of them were coming from church. They even hit a man was just out of the hospital and crippled with his wife leading him around the streets. Hit him on the head, split his head open. Then they went to the Atlantic House [a hotel], and passing the Atlantic House, a fellow jumped up there and the proprietor sitting on the verandah who was an invalid—they jammed him up against the building, hit his brother-in-law over the head. And the marks of the horses' shoes was on that verandah for years.

BERNIE GALLAWAY, SR.: After we were married—we were married one day and the strike came off the next—we stayed at my mother-in-law's a week or so. And Sunday evening [July 1] we went to church—the Polish church. And after we came out of church, we came down Victoria Road and when we got down where we lived—we lived right by the subway that used to separate this side from the Pier [the over-

pass today]—when we got there we decided to just keep on walking. So when we got by the railroad we saw this bunch of horses coming. Men on horseback—provincial police—with sticks, something like a baseball bat. I don't know how many there were. They lined up, they were coming down Victoria Road going towards the Pier. They were this side of the Pier. They got past us and her brother and his wife were behind us. And when we turned around to look, they were jumping over the fence.

ANASTASIA GALLAWAY: Those thugs were swinging those billies, you know, hitting the people. Beautiful Sunday evening after church and crowds of people walking, as we were doing. Beautiful Sunday summer's evening.

BERNIE: They were coming down in formation—but when they got past us, down to where the railroad track crossed the road at that time—they opened out on both sides, started galloping the horses and swinging those sticks at the people. Men and women.

ANASTASIA GALLAWAY: And when we looked, my brother

99

and his wife were going over the great big company fence, high as that. He was up and he had his wife by the hand, trying to drag her up over the fence where she wouldn't get hurt. There was a hotel over just the other side of the subway, and they drove the horse right in the front door of the hotel, right to the foot of the stairs, chasing the people. My sister-in-law's father was standing in the door—an elderly man—and the fellow come up and struck him and split his head open.

BERNIE: And they were doing that to force the men back to work, keep them in subjection, keep them down. Keep us all down.

MRS. GALLAWAY: We lived right on the front street, my mother did. She was at the front window, looking out. And they were down on the street. And one of them put up a gun to her, like that, and he told her to get in that window. And all this was against people not interfering with anyone or anything, walking after church—walking up the sidewalk on Victoria Road, on the right hand side because there was no sidewalk on the left hand side.

CHIEF OF POLICE, in the *Sydney Post*, 1923: "This stuff is all bunk. I know these people personally, and saw many of them heckling the police and throwing stones both before and after the troops. Now they have got what they have been itching for, and a lot of them want to fall back upon the plea that they were coming from church. Perhaps it was unfortunate that the charge should have taken place just at the time church was coming out, but at that I don't think many church people got mixed up in the raid."

Here is how the *Halifax Chronicle* reported these events:

At 8:45 p.m. a small body of provincial police moved out on foot and requested the crowd to disperse as the Riot Act had been read and the soldiers might be summoned. The belligerent section of the crowd replied with shouts of "yellow," "rats," "scabs," and other epithets, and proceeded to resist the advance of the police.

At this moment the mounted squad of provincial police, under Col. E. W. MacDonald, appeared suddenly at the city end of Victoria Road and charged the mob, using their batons freely. The crowd ran down into the nearby subway and up to the Whitney Pier end of Victoria Road.

Some of them resisted and engaged in hand-to-hand fights with the dismounted police.

The mounted police pursued the mob through the subway and into the alleys and by-ways of the Coke Ovens district, where many of them escaped in the pitch black maze of lanes which characterize that locality. Others were chased into the western part of ward five, right up to the residence of Mayor Fitzgerald.

During this charge of the police, many innocent by-standers received blows from the mounted men, because in the confined space it was of course impossible to tell who were strikers and who were spectators.

The first shots of the Sydney steel strike were heard last night at Whitney Pier, where things got so serious that the troops had to be called out, the Riot Act read, and a volley fired over the heads of the crowd in an effort to induce it to disperse. Even this show of military force seemed to have little effect and it was not until a machine gun was placed in position and preparation made to fire, that the mob moved slowly off and gave up its efforts for the night.

BERNIE GALLAWAY: And this is when the miners came out in sympathy with the steelworkers. Fellow by the name of Jim McLachlan brought them out. He was an old Scotchman, labour leader for years, and they say he learned most of his stuff down the mines in Scotland. And he came over here and he organized and he got to be a leader. He pulled the miners out.

EMERSON CAMPBELL: He said he would bring the miners out if we went out. And he was as good as his word. They called him everything. Said he was a Bolshevik, said he was Red. But he wasn't. He was just a hundred per cent pure labour man.

Maritime Labour Herald headlines:
MINERS STRIKE AGAINST USE OF TROOPS BY BESCO
•
ONE HUNDRED PER CENT STRIKE IS EFFECTIVE—
NO COAL BEING SHIPPED
•
BESCO CAN GET COAL
IF THEY REMOVE TROOPS THEY BROUGHT HERE

Views from the Steel Plant

Sydney Post:
GREAT BANKHEAD AT NO. 2
WITH ITS THREE HUNDRED TONS OF COAL IS ON FIRE
AND THE REQUEST OF VICE PRESIDENT MCDOUGALL
FOR MEN TO FIGHT THE BLAZE WAS CURTLY REFUSED
BY J. B. MCLACHLAN, WHO WOULD WILLINGLY SEE
THE WHOLE BANKHEAD GO UP IN SMOKE

The strike is to be one hundred per cent effective, which means that all maintenance men will be withdrawn. Company officials will take over the maintenance work and attempt to keep the pumps, fans and powerhouses in operation to save the mines. Bands of miners as pickets mounted guard around the collieries at midnight.

J. B. McLachlan issued this Official Letter, District 26, United Mine Workers of America, Glace Bay, July 6, 1923:

This office has been informed that all the Waterford, Sydney Mines and Glace Bay subdistricts are out on strike this morning as a protest against the importation of Provincial Police and federal troops into Sydney to intimidate the steelworkers into continuing work at 32 cents per hour.

On Sunday night last these provincial police, in the most brutal manner, rode down the people at Whitney Pier, who were on the street, most of whom were coming from church. Neither age, sex nor physical disabilities were proof against these brutes. One old woman over 70 years of age was beaten into insensibility and may die. A boy nine years old was trampled under the horses' feet and had his breastbone crushed in. One woman, beaten over the head with a police club, gave premature birth to a child. The child is dead and the woman's life despaired of. Men and women were beaten up inside their own homes.

Against these brutes the miners are on strike. The government of Nova Scotia is the guilty and responsible party for this crime. No miner or mine worker can remain at work while this government turns Sydney into a jungle; to do so is to sink your manhood and allow Armstrong and his miserable bunch of grafting politicians to trample your last shred of freedom on the sand. Call a meeting of your local at once and decide to spread the fight against Armstrong to every mine in Nova Scotia. Act at once—tomorrow may be too late.

102

Sydney Post, regarding McLachlan's letter:

Many of the men who obeyed the call of the executive of the United Mine Workers to strike in sympathy with the steelworkers of Sydney are beginning to realize their emotions were played upon by the circulation of false statements regarding the actions of the provincial police in Sydney.

It has not been proved that any of the incidents recorded above actually took place. And, furthermore, it is not surprising that men should strike when such an appeal to passion is made, and a tremendous revulsion of feeling may be expected when the miners find how low their best and manliest sentiments have been appealed to by a series of falsehoods and recital of incidents of which no record can be found, of which no actual witness of the crimes outlined have adduced.

Maritime Labour Herald:

The strike of the miners is not a wage strike. It has nothing to do with the contract that the corporation maintains exists between the miners and the companies. It is a strike for the defense of the workers against the armed troops sent here to force men to work for low wages. It is a strike called to protect the labour movement from the attacks of the capitalists and their government forces. The great phrases of "liberty," "freedom," and "constitutional rights," seem to have been forgotten when the profits of the British Empire Steel Corporation were in danger of being reduced through granting a slight increase in wages to the steel workers....

Chief McCormick of the Sydney police, asked by the *Post* if the troops should be removed from Sydney, said: "Such action at the present time would be the height of folly.... The mobs of striking steelworkers were never absolutely under control until the provincial police arrived on the ground, and even then they defied until orders were given to the mounties to charge into the rioting crowds. There is only one way to meet force of this kind and that with counter force. The best evidence that the Attorney General of Nova Scotia acted wisely in sending the police here is the fact that since the mounties charged and batoned the mob there has been peace and quiet in the strike district."

Sydney Post, July 5, 1923:

Further battalions of troops from as far west as Ontario and Manitoba are en route to Sydney and the strike area to the south. For what purpose, it is asked when there have not been any riots here or in the colliery districts during the present week.

The answer is that the mines of the Dominion Coal Company are rapidly filling with water, and should immediate assistance be not obtained millions of dollars worth of valuable property is in danger of being rendered worthless through flooding of the pits.

True there is no trouble at the mines for the simple reason that the strikers have things all their own way. They have driven maintenance men from all the pits leaving only inexperienced officials and other "white collar" volunteers to man the pumps and fans. At Dominion No. 2, perhaps the most costly equipped and most valuable colliery in the world, a little band of volunteers has been working night and day in an effort to keep the water from rising, but despite their most strenuous efforts the tide is going against them.

Sydney Post:
SENSATIONAL ARREST OF U.M.W. LEADERS

J. B. McLachlan, Secretary, and Dan Livingstone, President of the United Mine Workers of America, District 26, were arrested late last evening at Glace Bay U.M.W. headquarters, by chief of police J. B. McCormick, acting on instructions received from Hon. W. J. O'Hearn, Attorney-General of Nova Scotia, by telegram.

The move was wholly unexpected. No opposition was raised by the two men who quietly accompanied the chief to the city, where they spent the night in jail.

The charge under which the men were apprehended was that of publishing false news whereby injury is likely to be occasioned to the government and provincial police of Nova Scotia, contrary to section 136 of the criminal code.

The charge presumably arises out of the publication of a circular letter alleged to have been sent to the different locals by the U.M.W. executive, charging the provincial police with a series of crimes committed during raids made last week-end in Sydney. This is an indictable offence and those guilty of it are liable to a punishment of one year's imprisonment.

And the *Sydney Post* again:
Optimists here are of the opinion that the arrest of the leaders would

throw the miners into a panic and they would stampede back to the pits, but later developments are that the incarceration of the two prime movers in the sympathetic strike has cemented the ranks of the strikers more closely than they have been....

At a mass meeting of 4,000 miners held in Glace Bay Saturday evening and a similar large gathering of strikers held in the town of New Waterford yesterday afternoon, resolutions were passed protesting against the arrest of Dan Livingstone and J. B. McLachlan.... The meetings were wildly enthusiastic, and the strikers were urged by the speakers not to return to work until such time as their leaders have been released from custody and the charge against them withdrawn....

John L. Lewis, international president, came in for a stiff raking over at the meeting. The strikers were urged to pay no attention to Lewis's order to call the strike off, and it was declared by several of the speakers that if the international executive sent an investigating commission to Cape Breton the miners would throw them out....

The strike entering upon its second week shows no break in the solidarity of the men, that is, the strikers, although not wishing to see the fight a long one, show no disposition to return to the pit unless that return is unanimous.

ANDREW MERKEL, *Canadian Press staff writer*:

The most striking impression one receives upon being swept into the maelstrom of the conflict is the vehemence with which the miners believe that everybody's hand is against them. This is fundamental. One mentions the newspapers—"to hell with the newspapers"; the minister of labour—"To Hell with Murdock"; their own international leader—"To Hell with Lewis." The deep underlying reason for this state of mind I found to be the persistent spreading, day in and day out, of "false tales," to the discomfort of the men.

The coal pile at Dominion Number two is reported to be in imminent danger of destruction. Investigation shows it to be in no abnormal danger of destruction. The mines are reported to be rapidly filling with water. Investigation shows that they are not rapidly filling with water. Five thousand miners hear their leaders speak. Next day they find that words have been put into the mouths of their leaders which they know were never uttered. This sort of thing happens every day. When I told a group of young ministers in U.M.W. headquarters, Glace Bay, that the newspapers of Canada wanted an absolutely impartial account of the situation, I was promptly hooted and backed into a corner by a small forest of menacing hands. "To Hell with the newspapers."

I questioned J. B. McLachlan closely regarding the statement "To Hell with the property of the Dominion Coal Company," he is credited with having made at the conference with Hon. D. A. Cameron, the provincial secretary of Nova Scotia. He said:

"I am morally certain I did not make that statement, in so many words. There was a crowd there. Some one else might have made it. What I have said before and what I might have said at the meeting was, 'when you put the property of the Dominion Coal Company in one scale and the wives and children of workers earning thirty cents an hour, in the other, then I say to Hell with the property of the Dominion Coal Company.'"

EMERSON CAMPBELL: We steelworkers didn't know anything. Snap of your fingers, you got up in the morning and John L. Lewis was here in Cape Breton. He was president of the international union. He came from the U.S. to demote Jim McLachlan and put Silby Barrett in his place as president. He turned the charter of District 26 to the wall, revoked the charter. He told McLachlan, "You can't support the steelworkers. You've got a contract and your contract is still in force—you violated your contract," which he did, of course.

So John L. Lewis broke the strike.

BERNIE GALLAWAY: You see, John L. Lewis said you shouldn't have any sympathetic strikes—and he revoked the charter from Jim McLachlan and he set up a new slate of officers. And one of the fellows he set up was Silby Barrett—and he was a real arch-enemy of Jim McLachlan. McLachlan was considered too radical. Barrett took over and that was the end of the strike. I went to a meeting. I was still in the mines at that time. And there was a steel-worker there. And they told him to tell the steelworkers that now we're broke, that we can't do a damn thing to help you fellows now, the charter is revoked and we've got no strength. Go and tell the steelworkers that the strike is broke—but some other day, he says, we'll come back again. And that was the end of the whole thing. The miners were gone and that was it. And that was the breaking of the sympathetic strike, as they call it.

We continued on strike, but we couldn't make it without the miners. Your biggest trouble was you had men in the plant that didn't want to strike, they were anti-union and they kept working. Scabs we used to call them. Crawl underneath the fence and get in. Later on, I worked with a man in the acid plant and he told me he got a mattress in and he put it in a shed and he stayed there all the time the strike was on, working in the Steel Plant. So you had those to contend with. And then on the other side you had strikers who were provoking things. Strikers used to come in and take the foremen—which is wrong, because the foreman's not in the union and he's not in the strike—but they'd come in and take the foreman and parade him up the street. I knew an old Englishman, my boss, he was a chemist—he was an old, old man then, pretty near 75—and they took him and paraded him up Victoria Road. So one was sometimes as bad as the other. Because we were weak, we had no real organization.

[With the miners forced back to work, the steelworkers tried to hold out. They called a mass meeting in Whitney Pier, July 21.]

DAN MACKAY: You were not allowed to hold a meeting anywhere. I remember myself going down to a meeting, the only place we could have it was in Father Viola's field down at the Pier, because he had a place fenced around there and we were off the street. So we got in there and we held our meeting. The minute we came out of the meeting onto the sidewalks, the soldiers were there on horseback, about 50 of them. The officer commanding them gave them the orders, "Forward march, half right, half left."

Anyone who knows anything about military orders knows what would happen: 25 horses went to the right and 25 horses went to the left, and there was no chance in the world for anyone to escape except jump the fence and get away, some of them. They chased them for hours that day. Finally, some soldier hit a fellow in the side of the face with the side of his sabre. They all carried their sabres. The fellow fell down. No sooner did he fall than someone on our side threw a brick at this soldier and he dropped off his horse. Well, then the fat was in the fire.

EMERSON CAMPBELL: When we left that meeting back of the Italian church [at the Pier], the president of the union and I were left there together—that was Jack MacIntyre and I. But when we came up from the church there were two horses right on each side of us. And MacIntyre, he was always quick tempered, and he said, "Look, I'm going to grab [him]"—somebody would have been dead. I said, "No, Jack, don't." And the horse's nose right in my face till I got to the door here. He had the horses' nose right over my shoulder there, and him up there on top, you know, waving the billy. I went in at my house and then the two of them followed Jack MacIntyre home.

Sydney Post:
STEEL STRIKERS REQUESTED TO
VACATE CORPORATION HOUSES
Families must move so that residences may be available for loyal workers of company. Already, three eviction notices have been served to strikers living in company houses on Victoria Road, but these three tenants are being expelled for causing annoyance to some of their neighbours who are at work.

August 2, the steelworkers met and passed a resolution of capitulation. *Sydney Post* again:
STEELWORKERS VOTE UNCONDITIONALLY
TO RETURN TO WORK,
REALIZING THAT COMPANY HAS TRIUMPHED IN STRUGGLE
Whereas machine guns, bayonets, and provincial police have been used to cow us;... Whereas the press has also suppressed the news to further the unjust and untrue statements made of us;... Whereas our funds have been exhausted and some of our lower-paid members driven back to work;...

Be it resolved, therefore, that we return to work, although none of our grievances are disposed of, but on the contrary, are carried on to the future, although many of our best members will probably, as in the past, be unable to obtain work in Cape Breton and so must leave this country....

The 1923 Steel Strike

Sydney Post:
RADICAL WORKMEN,
BEATEN AT EVERY ANGLE
IN FIGHT WITH BESCO,
ASK FOR OLD POSITIONS
The management of the Dominion Iron & Steel Company issues the following statement:... Because of the reduction in the orders on the books of the company at this time, it will not be possible to employ as many men on the plant as were employed before the strike.

EMERSON CAMPBELL: That was the time I was blacklisted. They wouldn't take me back on the plant. And every week that I was off I had my wages come to the door here from fellows on the plant. I was better off than when I was working. But that is something, now, isn't it? Now I'm not blowing, but that is something. Every week the fellows would come up, "Here, Emerson"—$19 I think I was getting at that time. They had paid dues into the union, collected it amongst themselves.

BERNIE GALLAWAY: After that 1923 strike was over—the bosses took advantage of you, of all the workers, because they lost the strike. If you were active they'd give you the dirty end of the stick in any job there, they wouldn't give you justice. Give things to the fellows that weren't active. And blacklisting—Doane Curtis was a great labour leader in his day. He had to go to the States to get a job. There was Jack MacIntyre. He never went back on that plant. And a man named Murphy was very active—Jim Murphy— he had to go to the States—they wouldn't let him back on the plant. Paul MacNeil, he was blacklisted. He was a young man. He went down to Gary, Indiana, and he was only down there about a year when he was killed in an explosion in the Blast Furnace.

For a lot of men to get back on the plant you had to make a sweetheart agreement, which meant you weren't going to take any more active part [in the union].

Views from the Steel Plant

EMERSON: And when I did get back on the plant, they put me in Purgatory—put me on the back shift for a year. Gave me a labour job in the billets. But I walked around with my shoulders back and my head up. And after all that time in Purgatory, I'll have no trouble when I get to St. Peter's gate—I'll go straight in.

BERNIE: After the 1923 strike, there was no union. There was a union—a part of a union, you might say—but it was more of a company thing. Here in Sydney they called it the Bischoff Plan, because Bischoff was a head man of the plant at that time. That's how much of a union it was. It was really a company union. Used to have meetings, you know, and you'd have representatives—and you might get what you want and you might not. But you had no strength, no, no. I was never on the committee, but the committee even had their meetings in the General Office, that was the meeting place they had. The General Office of the plant itself. That's how much of a real union it was.

I think the pay I got at that time was 33 cents an hour. We worked—on day shift, anyone was working in the yard—we worked only 10 hours. But then when you'd get on a regular job you still had the 11 worked by day and 13 by night. You'd work for a week 11 hours a day—that'd be on a day shift. Then the next week I'd go to night shift. Well, then I'd work 13 hours each night. And every second week we'd work 24 hours through. That'd be on a Sunday. That'd be how you'd change over to the other shift. Stay at the plant for 24 hours. You might get a chance to go home and get a bite to eat, but your buddy would have to do your work for you when you were gone. Then he'd go and you'd have to do your own work and your buddy's too. They were terrible hours. The lowest rates. Used to bring home $19 a week.

(*Was the company union any good?*) Oh no. Well, you could go down on the plant and get up a load of wood. And then you'd get cheap coal—go in the office and get a ticket for coal. But apart from that, what you got in concessions you lost in wages. But from that 1923 strike, I learned this: that if the workers are going to get anywhere they've got to fight for it. They aren't going to sit on their fanny and get it. I figured that then and I figure it even today.

110

CHAPTER 5

The Coming of the Trade Union Act, 1937

After the 1923 strike and the coal miners' sympathy strike, the Plant Council—known as the Bischoff Plan, named after a BESCO manager at the Steel Plant—was the closest thing the Sydney steelworkers knew of union for the next fourteen years (1923 to 1937). And when they did finally achieve recognition of a union of their own, that recognition came via a mechanism won in a different kind of fight from the one that everyone expected. This mechanism was won politically, using the threat of the workers' vote at the polls. The mechanism was the Trade Union Act of 1937—legislation which said that a company cannot arbitrarily ignore the existence of a workers' union. It was the first Trade Union Act adopted by any Canadian province.

George MacEachern—with Carl Neville and Dan MacKay—researched and drafted the Trade Union Act—Bill 92, "An Act Respecting the Rights of Employees to Organize."

GEORGE MACEACHERN: We got an independent union going [Independent Steelworkers' Union of Nova Scotia]. The guide was given to those of us who were militant by the Communist International. Their advice was that in plants where there was a

111

plant council, militants were to join the plant council and use it to build a union. And this was done pretty generally. When I got on the plant, and the election for plant council came up, I ran. And mind you, the workers generally knew what the plant council was. They had no illusions about it at all. In some departments the boss had to go around and ask the men to vote, you know, because they knew it was a useless bloody thing. So I got on the plant council and started to raise issues. Tried to get blacklisted men back on the plant, but I couldn't.

So then we raised the wage question with Sir Newton Moore; he was president of the corporation. And he told us that it wasn't a matter of more wages but how long they could afford to pay the 28 cents an hour they were then paying, and that we better be careful because there was talk in the board of directors about moving the plant to Three Rivers, Quebec. And on like this. And when we left that meeting I managed to corral three or four of the plant councillors. I said, "Are you prepared to go back and tell the workers that the situation is hopeless?" "What else can we tell them?" "Well, you can tell them that there's hope, but that you can't get it with just discussion with the boss."

So I invited them up to the house. Four came. We chewed the thing over. We decided all we could do was go out and ask the men flat out, would they support a union. And if they would, we'd build a union for them, give leadership. And we'd meet the next Thursday night at my house. And the next Thursday only one fellow arrived—his name was Harry Davis, a Newfoundlander. Harry and I waited till 9 o'clock. No sign of anybody else. What are we going to do? We'll try it ourselves. So we decided that Harry would act as president, I would act as secretary.

Next day I took the day off and went out to Glace Bay to get union cards and dues stamps printed at Brodie's. Get minute books, financial books, call a meeting. And we did, and we got a pretty good turnout—50 or 60 came. That was encouraging. Of course on the percentage basis that wouldn't be big. But according to our expectations it was big. And we decided to continue organizing. If we had more experience I guess we would have put in wage demands and rallied the workers around a set of demands. But of course we weren't experienced. And on the day our next meeting was held, the plant council was called in and given a 10 per cent increase in wages—after Sir Newton Moore telling us with tears in his eyes no more than a month before that it wasn't possible, the company would sink.

We got a 10 per cent and two $7^{1}/_{2}$ per cent increases from the Steel Plant—we didn't even ask for them. It came through the plant council, see. But the union was responsible. The very fact that it was alive was responsible for those raises. We grew and they tried to head us off through the plant council. This was in 1935.

So we kept up our efforts—slow, tedious work—and did get up to 660 members. We were the Steelworkers Union of Nova Scotia. Other unions were springing up, and we were all in communication and had in mind the forming of a Canadian federation of steelworkers. The Amalgamated Association had broken down. Was it 4000 or 8000? One is as bad as the other. We weren't going to affiliate with that. Trades and Labour Congress of Canada didn't want us. They said our proper place was with the Amalgamated Association.

In the meantime R. B. Bennett, Prime Minister of Canada, had come out with a program which included the eight-hour day. Probably more sensible people wouldn't have bothered with it, because the federal government could only have the eight-hour day applied to federal employees. But that didn't bother us any. We took out a petition and took it around the plant, different departments. Some of the plant—the portions in continuous operation—had gone on the eight-hour day. There was no knowing when the others would get it. We formed a committee—didn't call it the union—and by-passed the plant council and got a meeting with Kelly. We asked him when we were going to get the eight-hour day. "First place, you'll get the eight-hour day when we're good and ready to give it to you. And in the second, I'm not talking to a bunch of gate-crashers"—and he walked out.

Fine. What better could you ask for when you're trying to build a union.

We got a good response to petitions and then called a meeting for a Saturday night in the Temperance Hall in Sydney. Our planned speaker couldn't come. By chance, Jim McLachlan and Annie Buller were giving an election talk. So they came down. Wonderful speakers. We had a packed meeting, good meeting. And there was another good meeting Sunday night. And Monday morning Kelly sent word to the plant council, he wanted a meeting, to tell them what he wouldn't tell us the week before—when they would get the eight-hour day. And you can depend that the union meetings forced this. The very fact that Jim MacLachlan and Annie Buller were addressing a meeting was enough to frighten hell out of them.

By this time, in 1936, the CIO [Congress of Industrial Organizations] had caught hold in the United States. There was a wonderful enthusiasm. But John L. Lewis wasn't too fussy about moving into Canada because, well, they didn't have the apparatus to move in. They were having a hell of a tough time with the employers in the U.S.

The CIO steelworkers, SWOC [Steel Workers Organizing Committee], was set up in Hamilton. A fellow by the name of Ernie Curtis who had been in the 1923 strike here—I wrote to him and I got credentialed as an organizer. Then Carl Neville, by this time he became president of the union—Harry Davis was hurt and couldn't continue. Carl and I went to a District 26 convention in Truro, asked for help, and was promised. They asked John L. Lewis to appoint Silby Barrett to help us—Silby was international board member for the U.M.W. at the time.

On the 13th of December we held our first meeting—now we were CIO, SWOC—started with 10 names. By March we must have had 3000 members. Oh, they just flocked. We hired halls all over town. Did it ourselves. Didn't cost the international a red cent. We had the little bit of money left over from the old Independent Union. We had really come to the crunch. We had a union but the company had a plant council. And I went down to the plant council and asked them to resign in a body and make way for the union. They were only holding things up. They wouldn't do it.

So at that stage it would have to be political. So Angus L. MacDonald, Premier of Nova Scotia, came to town on party business. We got a meeting with him. We convinced him there, if he wasn't already convinced, that we had to have a Trade Union Act or we had to have a strike of steelworkers and miners like in 1923. We had drawn up a bill based on the Wagner Act in the U.S. and the Coal Mines Regulation Act of Nova Scotia. We wanted recogni-

114

tion, wanted the check-off. We went after them on the political front. The act would say that the company could not fire you for belonging to a union, company would have to recognize the union once you could establish that you had a majority, company would have to provide you with a check-off of union dues once you had shown that you had a majority in favour.

Before he left, Angus L. said he couldn't promise it would be passed, but that it would be brought up. But he said, "I'm going to need support. Get public support for your bill." Which we did. We got really good support by means of petitions and resolutions. Took petitions to businessmen, professional men all around the industrial area. We contacted all the organizations we could think of. *Any* organization. The only organization that didn't endorse our resolution was the Sydney Board of Trade.

You can see the good that's in people when you think of the work they did in that union freely. And the signing up of union members—3000 members. Any number of people on the plant would take cards out, sign people up. Even today it's encouraging to think that people, once they've understood a thing and taken hold of it, can really move mountains. The businesses, as a body, disagreed with us, but as individuals they signed the petitions.

It was a rare time. Older, experienced people would have hesitated. But we didn't know better and just went after it. Going up to the Law Amendments Committee in Halifax, with our petitions and resolutions of the Trade Union Act, there was an old railway unionist on the train. We told him of our mission. He said, "Good God! Presumption born of ignorance. Do you really expect to get that? You must be crazy. Look, I remember when we tried to get automatic couplings. You know, we drank a whole bottle of Bobby Burns whiskey before we went to get automatic couplings instead of the old link-and-pin."

But we had lots of confidence. And we rode on a tide of success, all those people signed up. And you just think: all those broken strikes and broken unions, for people to go into one and particularly an international one—because some of those plant councillors had been in the 1923 strike and they were death against international unions. (*Well, they saw John L. Lewis break that strike;*

115

how could they trust him now?) That's right. (*Did you trust him?*)
Well, to be honest, I wouldn't have been surprised if he turned on
us, but he didn't. He had changed.

But poor Jim MacLachlan couldn't stand it. His position was,
John L. Lewis is no good and he'll never be any good, which is something less than Marxian. There is nothing permanent but change. But
Jim would have nothing to do with it. Jim had been badly hurt personally; he had lost his position with the UMW, blacklisted, he couldn't
go back in the mines after 1923—and he had a hate of John L. Lewis
and all that he stood for. Well, all that he stood for in 1923 could well
be hated, if you can hate. I felt Lewis had changed.

And I felt we *had* to trust him. We had no bloody choice there.
(*Do you think the business people came around because they felt*
they *could trust Lewis? After all, he had held the miners to their
contract in 1923.*) I never thought of it that way. I don't know that
the business community was that astute. (*And Jim MacLachlan felt
there were higher principles that might call for breaking a contract?*) That's right. Jim was a marvelous man. Principle was a big
thing with him. Well, the way he had to live for years and years
with a couple of cows and a little bit of a garden....

Anyway, we were one of the first unions in the entire international to be recognized by the company by virtue of this act. (*Was the
company bitter?*) Not much. See, they're businessmen. They depended
to a great extent on government handouts, always have—so they
weren't going to fight the government. The government didn't have
the fear of the union that big industry has. Big industry is less concerned about the dollar-and-cents things than it is about control, power.
And our unions, unfortunately, are no threat to this power. So our real
power in this was the threat of our vote at the polls.

(*So, when a union finally comes to the steelworkers at Sydney, it's
peaceful.*) Peaceful. Political. We steelworkers might have had all the
trouble others had and worse—if there wasn't an election just a couple
of months away. We had 3000 people organized. And in Trenton they
had the plant organized. And if we had to go on strike before election,
Angus L. was going to be in a bad way. The international nor the
people here could not support a strike. But we would have had no
other choice, and it would have been a bad repetition of 1923.

CHAPTER 6

Women in the Steel Plant, World War 2

Chris McGrady • Kit Falconer
Selina Hollohan • Mary Kelly
Dorothy Dobranski • Erma Maxwell
Kay Henrich

CHRIS McGRADY: The main reason I applied was that when my husband went overseas, we had four children. And at that time they were only paying for two children. We were getting a princely sum

of $12 a month per child. And I think the total we were getting was about $79 a month—total. Jimmy went overseas in 1941. I was living at home with my parents. Then after my father died in September 1942, it wasn't all that easy. I went working at the plant. Then in '43, I think, they started paying for four children. I think we got around—with the cost of living—I think it came up to about $91 a month.

And that's what we were getting up until the time Jimmy came home in 1945. That's less than $25 a week. Can you imagine! And that included everything—feed your children, look after them. If I didn't go to work, you know, what else was there?

And many more women went to work. Not all for the same reasons; but you know, they felt it was their patriotic duty to release a man for service.

(*Who cared for the children while you worked?*) Oh, my mother. Well, you know, I wouldn't let my mother look after them to *that* extent. She was here with them and she guided them, but as far as washing for them or cooking for them or getting them lunch or something—because, when I came home from the Steel Plant, I used to have to go to the store and pick up the groceries, and come home and cook the dinner and do their laundry and everything like this. 'Cause I wouldn't allow my mother to do that. (*It must have been hard.*) Well, I was a lot younger then. I didn't mind it that much.

KIT FALCONER: (*Were you married then?*) No. (*Were you working?*) Oh, yeah. I worked housework, restaurants, I worked for a dairy, different things. You name it. I was living with my family, but I was paying my way. After all, we've got to work. There wasn't anything, really, for a woman— only restaurants or housework or something similar to that, that's all. Doing the dirty work.

(*Were you surprised that the Steel Plant was hiring women?*) Really, I was. But when I heard they were, I just took the opportunity. I said, Well, that's for me. I'm going to put my name in, and if I can get a job, I'm going to work.

(*Was there any chance of a future there?*) No. You'd just be on there till a certain time. Once men were coming back, there'd be jobs for them, and they wouldn't require girls. (*Did they tell you that when you were hired?*) Oh yeah, we knew that; it wouldn't be permanent or anything like that. (*Did you ever wonder whether that was just?*) Well, not really. Just wanted a job for the time being, and just left it at that. As long as it went, fine, and if you got laid off, well.... (*So you weren't concerned whether it was fair or not.*) Not really, no. I think it's a man's job, and when they haven't got the men, if women can replace them for the length of time that they need them, fine. (*It was never a question of, if we can do it, we should be allowed to do it.*) No, no.

SELINA HOLLOHAN: I always lived with my parents, and I worked in town—at a clothing store on Charlotte Street. And then from there I went to the plant. (*Why did you change?*) More money.

I was contributing to my family, my whole pay. I wouldn't take anything. My mother was very sick with cancer. And my dad had to stay home quite a bit. So at that time I used to take two

119

dollars out of my pay, and I took my pay to my father or my mother. But they were so good, they were such *good* people, that I was really happy that I could do it.

(*Do you have any idea how you heard about the Steel Plant?*) Everybody around worked at the plant, the men. And at the time, during the war, there was a shortage of men. So they were hiring women. So I tried to get on. It took me a long time to get on, though. You know, you had to have drag then, too. I didn't have it. My family didn't work at the plant. My father ran a business on Charlotte Street.

(*So you went and you applied, but you weren't taken right away?*) Oh, no. I walked back and forth there till I wore a pair of shoes out, I always say. They'd just say that there was no opening yet, and put you off like they do for every other job. And finally, I got on. But I got on through—I went to see the priest in our church. And he made a phone call. I was trying about four or five months, and I couldn't do *anything* on my own. Finally, I went to him, and he made a phone call, and he was pretty mad about the whole thing, because he had known so many others that did get on that didn't even need it. So that's the way I got on.

(*You worked at the Coke Ovens?*) That was the first job I got on the plant, and I just stayed there for 14 months. I was breaking doors and cleaning mud, and mudding doors, and cleaning the walk. You know, the old mud would fall off the doors, so you had to clean that in a wheelbarrow, take it down to the end. It was dirty, that's all. You got the smell of the gas and that. Which wasn't very good, really. A person—like, a woman couldn't stay there for too long a time. But I stayed there for 14 months.

(*Do you think it was because you were Lebanese that you had trouble getting on the plant?*) No, I don't think that that had too much to do with it. I don't think. There were a lot of coloured girls got on the plant. There were a lot of foreign. I think, myself, that it was just the fellow who was doing the hiring. He'd just pick and choose. (*Although, it's been said to me of coloured girls, that the only job they ever got on the plant was on the Coke Ovens.*) Yeah. That's the only job I got, too.

I liked it, though. (*Did you find the work hard?*) Not too bad. I had a boyfriend there after a while, so it got a little easier. 'Cause he used to take the heavy cart for me, and that. You know, the wheelbarrow filled with mud, which wasn't very light. If he was off on his lunch hour, he'd do that for me. (*I understand the job was an hour on and an hour off.*) Because you see, it's all hot, hot as the devil. I mean, you couldn't work it right through, you couldn't. It was too hard. You'd flop. Oh, it was a real tough job.

DOROTHY DOBRANSKI: My father and all my uncles had always been part of the Steel Plant. My grandfather was J. C. Mackley. He was the general superintendent of the Blast Furnace for years and years and years. And then, all my uncles worked. My father was the general foreman for the Electrical Department. And then one time my uncle, George Mackley, was master me-chanic up at the Coke Ovens. The Mackleys have always held good positions in the plant. No doubt it was through them, through my father mostly, that we knew there was a possibility. I have an idea that my father must have approached somebody in the lab at first. But I had graduated from college as a home economics teacher. I had taught at Holy Angels High School for a year, and then in the rural areas for another year, and then on this circuit from Sydney River to St. Peter's. So it was very interesting to me to get a job, to be able to stay home. And besides that, I had always liked chemistry, and it was a chance to do that. The teaching jobs were not available.

The plant wasn't that foreign to me, because I had often been back and forth with my father. Not exactly in the area that I went to, in the chem lab up at the Coke Ovens. But it was so very much like a chem lab in college that it wasn't scary at all. And we were given a lot of instruction. We spent two weeks, I believe it was, with the men on the job. And then they were moved down to the big lab, down to the main lab. And we were left alone after two weeks.

They had one girl on each shift. We were analyzing the products of the distillation plant—what they called the benzol plant. We did mostly fractional distillations. The operation there in the benzol was a huge big still, where they were taking off the by-products of the oil. And in order to do that, they have to separate the different substances by their boiling point.

They would bring a sample in to us, and we would have to put it on the distillation apparatus and get the boiling point—the first drop would come over at a certain point. That temperature was very, very important to the man who was operating the still. He would know whether he would have to change tanks of where the solution was running. Then, when they would fill a tank, we would have to analyze that again. That's what fractional distillation is— it's separating all the different substances within the liquids that come off the by-products of coal.

(*Was it dangerous work?*) Well, we didn't think so at the time. There were a lot of precautions we had to take. We had to realize we were working with inflammable liquid at all times. And no-body was allowed to come in the lab at all. There were three shifts operating. On dayshift, people would be around. But on the middle shift and the backshift, we were just by ourselves in the lab. And the samples were brought in to us, and passed in through the door. We would analyze them, and put the results out on a paper for the operator in the plant. So we were quite on our own.

When I was there, one of the men died because he was over-come by fumes, when one of the big huge stills overflowed. There would be just one man looking after that end, and one man looking after the other small still. And they wouldn't see one another that much during the night. And when I came out to work this morning, all the commotion that was going on because he had been found dead. So, I went through that. It was rather scary. It made us realize that the fumes of the product we were working at—if in quantity and inhaled under any circumstances—it could be dangerous. There was no smoking allowed in the lab where we were working, at all.

And this is one of the reasons why my parents felt it was a very safe place to work. There were so few people. And the fact of all this security, due to the flammability of the product. In one way, it was dangerous, what you were working at. But if all the rules were kept, that was all right.

(*Were your parents in support of your work?*) Oh yes, yes. It wasn't so unique at that time. Like, some of the women who were working—we used to watch the women out the lab window who worked over around the Coke Ovens cars. And they had to wear asbestos suits and asbestos gloves, and they were sorting the coal as to sizes. Well, see, we weren't involved in any of that.

Our biggest problem was getting back and forth to work, because the [regular] shift changed at 11 o'clock—[but] our shift changed at 12. So we'd have to get from Victoria Road into the benzol plant, which was quite a dark walk. We always had to make sure somebody was walking with you. Sometimes the watchman would come out and meet you, because it was very, very dark. That was one little bit of an inconvenience.

The man who came back to take my job, he had been a prisoner-of-war. And when he came back, they gave him his choice: Did he want to go to the main lab down at the plant, or back to his old job at the benzol lab? And he chose the benzol lab. So they offered me the job to go down to the main lab. But my father wouldn't let me do that. 'Cause I'd have to go through the whole plant to get to work, and it would be entirely a different type of an atmosphere that I would be working under. So, it was time to pick up my teaching again.

(*But did you* want *to go to the main lab?*) At the time, I sort of wanted to go. But it meant I would have to go down into the noisy, dirty end of the plant. In other words, disregarding my sex, I just had to fit in where I was on the seniority list. And that hurt me more—I felt, oh gee, they knew very well I couldn't do that. And even when I used to meet him and talk to him, I still felt that. And yet, how right he was—he's the one that went to war. He was the one that had the job before. And he's the one that had been the prisoner for three or four years. Everything rightfully belonged to him, and he made his career there. But I was a little bitter, 'cause I thought I was the one that should have been allowed to make the choice where I wanted to go.

But when the supervisors explained what would be expected of me, it was that business of having to go through the plant to get to work, and out again, more than the actual work itself. I loved the work. I loved doing the chemical analysis. So they asked me if I wanted to go to work in the lower lab. That I could have the job if I wanted to. But at the same time, they were saying it in such a way that I felt they didn't want me to go down there either. So I gave up.

ERMA MAXWELL: I didn't think I'd be actually doing the same work as the men. You know, I thought it was just small jobs.

Well, they told me I was going to be working on the batteries. That's at the Coke Ovens. We were working with the men, and they kind of showed us, showed the women. There were three on each side—there was the pusher side, and then there was the coke side—two sides to the battery. Usually, I worked on the coke side. (*What did you do there?*) The same as the men, you know—breaking doors, and mudding them. On both sides you did the same thing—break, mud, and pick up.

(*Which comes first?*) Breaking. They had this machine on the pusher side, this big machine. And it had this big contraption that went up to the door. The man that operated the machine pulled a lever and this thing went out and grabbed the top and the bottom of the door, and kind of shook it, because there was mud around it. And he'd take the door off. And then he'd pull it back, and move the machine. Then this other big steel thing would push the coke right through the ovens. On the coke side they had the hot car. The coke just came out and fell into the hot car that was on tracks. And then it would go down to what you call the quencher station. When he drove in there, the water came down and it would quench the coke. Because it was red hot, coming out. And sometimes, when the coke came out, it'd spill a bit. And we had to go then with a shovel and shovel it back in the oven. It might be just a couple of shovelfuls. Or sometimes they'll have what you call a spill. And then there'd be quite a bit that you'd have to shovel. (*Red hot?*) Oh yes, red hot.

Then they had what you call the mud truck, or the mud car. This thing was on tracks. Between Number 4 and Number 3 battery they had a big place—this man was inside there—he had a mixing machine. It was mud. And we had to bring the machine up to the door, and load it up with this mud. And after they put the door back on, then we had to come up with the mud truck. We had like a handle; what would you call it? (*Like a trowel?*) Yes. We'd take that and do the door, mud it all around, seal it, really. Then the old mud that had come off—the person with the wheelbarrow came behind, and they'd have to scrape up the old mud and put it in the wheelbarrow. And then they took it back into this place where this man was making the mud.

When you went down to load it up, it was very heavy, to shovel it. Especially when you had to load the top part of the mud truck. Sometimes the men would help. You know, if they were in the mood, they'd help you. (*And if they weren't?*) Well, you do it yourself.

You just won't believe how heavy that mud was. And you had to put enough on that truck to mud those—I just forget the amount of doors. (*Was this truck mechanized?*) No, it was something you pushed. It was on wheels, and you just pushed it along the track. Had to push it, from door to door, to mud each door.

Then there were some women that picked coke. After they quenched the coke, it used to go down this slide, and it would run up on this big conveyor belt. And the women used to be up, then, on each side. They used to pick coke. There were certain pieces that they were picking out. And sometimes the coke would spill off of this belt. Then we had to go down like on each side, and take this with a shovel and shovel this coke back up on the belt. And it used to be kind of wet and damp and things down there, you know, from off the coke.

But the mudding was really the hard part, to get the mud to stick on those doors. You know, there was a certain way you had to throw the mud, to get it to stick. And then you take it and level it off all around so the gas wouldn't seep out.

(*I guess you earned your money.*) Oh, I guess I did. I wasn't ashamed to put my hand out for my pay. At that time, for seven shifts, we were getting about $20.

My dad died shortly after I started. I don't think it was quite a year, when he died. It was nice at first, because he used to get up in the morning, 'cause he worked all day shift, too. And he'd get up in the morning and make my breakfast and wake me up, and both of us would have breakfast together. He worked down at the other end of the plant, down at the Foundry. And both of us would leave for work at the same time—he'd go out his way, and I'd go down to the Coke Ovens.

So, it was nice for a while. He was very proud of me, to know that I was working. Very proud.

CHRIS McGRADY: I went down and worked down in the lumber yard. I was foreman of the women. Probably they thought it was a better idea to have a woman foreman than a man, you know, over the women. And I was elected. And then I started checking lumber. What we were doing was really measuring the lumber, and stacking it. Then when the weather got sort of bad, we went in the warehouse. Well, of course, this was part of the lumber yard. Then I went down to the yard office. Then I was selling bonds on the plant, all over, whatever took in the General Yard. So I sold bonds there for a while. After the bonds were finished, we went down to the brick shed.

There were an awful lot down at the brick shed. We were just counting the brick, and piling the brick, and doing things like this.

But we didn't stay down in the brick shed very long. We came back. And we went upstairs in the warehouse, and we were doing some filing of the old ledgers and things like that. I didn't find it all that terrible.

Gwen Andrews tying a reel of wire

KIT FALCONER: I worked in the Bar Mill—bundling bars. You'd put so many in a bundle—and I used to have to count them. Sometimes it'd be over a hundred. There'd be three people on what they call a bundling bed. And we'd have to tie wires on both ends and in the centre. Then I put the tag on them. When we'd get the whole thing set up, we'd call the crane, and then we'd have to place them. The crane would come and lift it. They had certain places to put them, on the floor. And we'd hold each end and place it, in the right position. (*You wouldn't take the weight of it.*) Oh no, no. But we'd have to go down with the crane, follow the crane down, and give him the directions to lower it—and we'd place it. Use your hands, signal.

Then another job we had was the reels. They came right from the furnace, from what they call the hot end. It's wire in reels. So, there'd have to be two girls there. You tie three wires on. We'd have to tie one on each side and one in the centre, and put the tag on. See, and we used to have to lift our foot up and kick them together, to tighten them, before we'd put the wire on. A girl on one side and one on the other. Oh, it was fun.

And then I worked on what they call a straightening machine. Now, that's bars that come up—some of them are a little bit off, or whatever. We'd just put them through the straighteners. Then, you'd have to look for rejects, you know, some of them that you'd have to throw away. There'd be slivers in it, or some of them wouldn't be as wide as the others—similar to that. It wasn't just a job of just tie something up. No, no. There was a little responsibility in all of it.

KAY RILEY HENRICH: Look, I enjoyed it so much. The men were all older, and they had known my father, because he too worked there. He was superintendent of carpenters within the mechanical department—and they all knew him. My father used to take us— we were three girls—used to take us Sunday after Mass—over to his shop and show us all around. We were quite familiar with the plant. I felt very secure there. It wasn't strange to me.

I was 16 when my father died. And they became very protective of me—they immediately became fathers and guardians to me. And then, I was so young when I went to work—I was 17.

There was one man, he used to come over every morning. Every morning he'd come over to my machine and talk to me, just to say hello. He knew my father so well, and used to check in and see if everything was all right, and everything I needed. They were so nice to me, very protective, as I say. Nobody ever passed the machine where I was working without stopping and saying hello, nobody. And at lunchtime, the man I worked with, he'd go down— they had this little store at Number 1 gate—he'd always come back and bring me an ice cream or something. They were so nice to me. Getting all the goodies. They were nice to all the women in the shop. I felt like a queen the whole time. I was never allowed to lift anything.

I was working on a gear-cutting machine. It was a huge machine, about twice the size of a tractor, say, and it was all mechanically set up to cut pinions and gears. You know what gears are, any kind of a gear. Like there's little gears in a watch, there are big gears on machines. This is a gear about two feet in diameter. And some of them a little smaller. And this pinion went on—it was all steel. You set up your machine for your cutter to cut through it. And it turned around, and would cut a tooth. Then it would turn around and cut another tooth. Into a gear.

(*Does it take any strength?*) No, no strength on my part. There was no manual labour to it. And for the men there'd be none, because these chain falls were set up overhead for you to lift the gears and put them in place. Once I had it set up, I just had to watch that the gears were cut. I was measuring the tooth, to make sure it was right. A caliper, in a sense, but not adjustable. I was like the machinist's helper. There were two machines, two gear-cutters—he worked on one, and I worked on the other. It was only probably three feet between each machine.

We dressed, of course, in jeans and sweater, like the rest of the men. We had to have our hair covered over for fear of catching our hair in machines. But at no time did we ever wear gloves. And one thing I did mind: I recall when I'd go to a dance—we'd go to dances as many nights as we could—I'd look at my hands and my fingernails, because we couldn't wear gloves, you know—my fingernails became full of grease that I couldn't get out. And I'd always sit with my hands like this [in fists]—because I could never get my hands clean. And working with machinery, splinters of metal would cut your fingers—chips from pinions. Not cut them deep, but scratch them, and the grease would get into this. And, look they weren't sore, but they didn't look the nicest. No matter how much cream or what have you, they were there. And I was always aware of my hands when I went to a dance.

(*Do you think this job changed your view of what women can do?*) Oh, yes. They can certainly fill in when there's no men. But to me, it's a man's job. As I said, I wouldn't want to spend my life there, that's for sure.

There were some ladies who were sweepers, they were older women, say, in their 50s. I remember this poor woman, she was a sweeper. There was a bench behind my machine, if anybody wanted to hide for a little nap. And they did. They'd come in there, and I'd watch. And this poor woman, she worked hard at home and she worked hard there. She worked there because she needed the money. And every now and then, she'd crawl in back and she'd fall asleep, and her head would go back and her mouth would open, she'd be snoring. And the men down there would say, "Is she asleep?" I'd say, "Yes." And they'd tap the pipes overhead, and all the rust would come down in her mouth!

She was probably a mother bringing up a bunch of children alone. This much I knew. She had a responsibility. Where I was a young unmarried girl, she was a mother with a bunch of children. She probably had to get up God knows when. Well, I left home at 6:10; we had to punch a clock in at 7 o'clock. Well now, see, my mother got me up, packed my lunch, and away I went. But this woman probably had to pack lunches for four or five kids, do a wash and hang it out. She worked hard at home before she even left, and went home and worked again. She was tired. Double work, yeah. There were several. There were a lot of ladies over there who were widowed and were just too glad to jump at the opportunity. 'Cause the money—when I say 59$^1/_2$ cents an hour, that doesn't sound like much, but it was good wages then. And this is why a lot of them worked there.

MARY KELLY: I worked at the Isle Royale Hotel in the dining room, and I had six children. I worked long hours, and I was a widow. And when I heard that they were taking women on, I went over and applied for the job, and I got it. I preferred working day shift because I wanted to be home in the evening with the children. Whereas, at the hotel, I had to work until 9 and 10 o'clock at night. Sometimes the children'd be in bed when I got home at night. (*When you worked at the Isle Royale?*) I wouldn't see them in the morning, or even then in the night. That went on for years. But, there was no other work.

Then I got at the safety department at the Steel Plant. And there was no night work—I had all day shift. The pay wasn't better. Our pay at the hotel was very poor, but our tips would amount to about the same. So, the reason was the shorter hours. (*Would you have to come home from the Steel Plant and do a day's work?*) Oh, yeah. Wash by hand. But I was young, see, you didn't mind it.

I started in the safety department. I had to cover the whole place, wherever the women were working, to see that they wore safety shoes, and their hair was tied up. They had to wear a bandanna. Some of the women didn't like to cover their hair, you know. And they were provided with nets. But they didn't like it. Some of them wouldn't. I'd have to report that to the boss. And no rings, no jewelry, that would get caught in anything. And gloves, like the men. Slacks weren't very prominent then, but a lot of them wore just the men's overalls, you know, for working. They weren't allowed to wear skirts.

And I also put safety posters up, pertaining to different hazards. Like a step: "Watch Your Step." And around lathes, you know, the picture of a man not wearing goggles—where he should have been wearing safety goggles. Every department had their own kind of a poster.

I didn't mind it a bit. And I liked going out around. I went all over the plant, every part of the plant. Right down from the docks right up to what they call the marsh dump—it was where they used to dump the old coal or something. Oh, I walked. I'd take one section one day, and another section, another, and so on. When I was outside, I was really my own boss.

And then after that, they took another man on, and I went in the store, selling safety equipment, all the goggles. Most of them were issued by the plant for safety purposes. Safety goggles and gloves. But they bought their safety boots.

(*And you stayed on the plant after the war.*) Oh, yes. When the women left, I went in the store. Then I stayed on till I had a heart attack in 1967. I was the only woman that was inside the plant. With the exception of a couple stenographers, you know. I was with DOSCO for 24¹/₂ years.

SELINA HOLLOHAN: They don't make them like us today. The women of today, they can't do half of what we used to do. When you think of what we used to do—my God! I raised seven children, and I used to do all my own work and pack my kids and walk down to my father's—my mother was dead—and I used to do his work. And bring my kids back home, and be home for supper, have my husband's supper ready. Today, they don't do things like that. I don't think so. Maybe there are some around, but I doubt it.

We did what men were supposed to be doing. Ordinarily, you'd never get on, if there was no war. And the men were all gone, so somebody had to hold up this end. I mean, maybe we didn't do a whole lot, but we held up our end at the plant, kept the plant going.

Selina Haddad Hollohan, Minnie Paruch,
Bernadette O'Neil Keough, and Lil

CHAPTER 7

Rose Grant Young, Crane Operator

I grew up right here in Whitney Pier. My mother was a MacDonald from Irish Cove. Now, they came to Sydney before the plant was built. And the old house that we lived in on Henry Street was taken down from Irish Cove on a scow. It was drifted right up, and they pulled it up over Henry Street hill with horses, and they put it where it's today still, on an angle from the Royal Bank. Then they built the front on it and they built a back on it and a side on it; and in the end, it's an enormous house. But that's the way it started.

Now, my Grandfather Grant, his name was Jim. And when I was on the plant, the older men told me that he was the best rigger they had. Of course, he was dead and gone years before I was born. A rigger is the man that does the knots and holds the swings and everything, gets everything ready for the lifts. All the knots and everything to hold all that heavy equipment. Of course, they're a climber, too, they have to climb. And of course, the Newfoundlanders were fishermen and they were good riggers, so there was an influx of Newfoundlanders after the plant was built. He came from St. John's. They rented or bought a house on the top of Henry Street, and my mother lived at the bottom of Henry Street. This is how they got together.

I was only born in '21. And we lived on the street where the gate to the Steel Plant was. It was a mainstream for everything there at the Pier. Because the bank was on the corner, all the shops were along, and the gate to the plant was right at the foot of the hill. In fact, when we were kids, I had a bobsled. And we used to take the men down over the hill on the bobsled to work in the wintertime—those that were brave enough to come with us!

(*Did you ever really have a desire to work on the plant?*) No. This was 1942, that I went on the plant. At that time, my mother was in financial difficulties. And I asked for a raise at the place where I was working, and I didn't get too much satisfaction. So when I heard that they were taking names on the plant—there were two of us, another girl whose father was dead, too, came with me. In fact, there were four of us out of this store. We went over and put our names in. But we didn't have a clue as to what we were going to do or anything. We really didn't think it over. As I say, we were only kids, really. Two of us were called, and the other two weren't. And I often thought afterwards, it was because we were the children of widows that we got the jobs ahead of the others. At least, that's the way it appeared. Or any women whose husband had worked on the plant and for some reason, through sickness or something like that, weren't working, they got the jobs, too.

Of course, towards the end, they were taking all the applications. Everybody was crying for steel, of course, during the war. Everything was swinging. We were working double shifts, triple shifts, everything to get the steel out. It was totally different. The Rail Mill was on two shifts practically all during the war. And then they rolled tie plate and the different type rails—the different pound-age, you know—and mine arches—where today they only have rail. Of course, they had markets for it. The mines were crying for the mine arches. Every section of the plant was working, working, working, all the time.

The superintendent in the department that I landed at—it was the Plate Mill—he told me, "They tell me a woman will never run the Rail Mill crane." And he said, "You and I are going to prove them wrong!" He was quite a psychologist. And of course, that's all I needed to hear, was that the men were against the women; in other words, that made me try that much harder. (*He felt that the men were not going to accept the women on the plant?*) Especially in the jobs overhead, where their lives were at stake, see. I carried an awful lot of tonnage above their heads. And they didn't have faith in the women.

I didn't have sense enough to realize what they were putting me into, to tell you the truth. First, they broke me in on the Pipe Mill cranes, which were wide open bays—in other words, there was no interference. They taught me how to use the magnet and the shifts and all the different things. But they were really getting me ready for the Rail Mill, without telling me that, see. I thought it was always going to be the long open bays, but it wasn't. (*By "a long open bay," that means...?*) That it's all open. It would be like the length of this street.

And perhaps they were scarfing the steel. Do you know what scarfing is? They take the flaws out of the steel, big chunks of steel; and I'd have to turn them over so they could take the flaws out of them. Things like that.

But then they took me to the Rail Mill. And he told me, "Now, this is what we've been getting you ready for." He said, "This is the one mill that we always make a dollar on." That was the way he described it to me. But he took me to the foot of the ladder, and he said, "You'll have to go the rest of the way yourself." He was an electrical engineer, and he was scared of height. (*You didn't operate this from the ground?*) Oh heavens, no, I was overhead. Twelve feet, I suppose. All the workings of the crane were on top of the crane. We had to oil them every day and get ready for the shift.

Which meant that I'd have to go to perhaps 15 feet. (*You not only operated the crane, then, you were responsible for maintaining it.*) Oh, yes, for oiling it and seeing that it worked. Now, if anything went wrong with the crane, like the fingers—we had the old-fashioned boxes. I suppose you wouldn't even remember the old tram cars, they had the box-type levers. And it's like a finger that makes the connection.

But anyhow, as I said, he was scared of heights, so I had to go the rest of the way by myself. But this man, Maynard, they gave me to him to break me in—he was a fantastic operator. He had been there for 35 years. He taught me how to pick up the boxes with the scrap in, take it down, dump it, bring it back. Of course, they were all old men, remember that—all the young fellows were gone. And this old crane-chaser that I had—he must have been 85 then—I think he lived till he was 100! But anyhow, to save him walking the whole length of the mill, this is what Maynard used to do: he used to dump the boxes, and he taught me how to catch them back up again and bring them back so that that poor old fellow didn't have to walk all that distance. Well, I thought it was part of the job.

He also taught me so many things about the lifts; you know, when you get the lift up, to keep it from swaying, and things like that. Another thing he taught: this great big enormous screw on top of the housing—they had to tighten that to hold all the things in the housing for the rails to come through, so they wouldn't move, so there wouldn't be any bumps in the rail. But Maynard used to take the big hook—a great big enormous thing—we had two hooks on our crane—and he used to sway that hook, and he could tighten with those hooks so the men didn't have to hammer that screw down. Save the men the work. When the men were standing on the top of the housing, they could almost touch the cab of the crane, they were that high up. But he would use that, and he would pound it. Well, he taught me that. And I thought it was part of the job. I never realized that he was making a show-off of me.

Because later, I discovered, everybody used to stand and just watch, and they were in awe of the things I could do, with the straps. Now, we'd take hot steel—and the steel things were about

A view inside the Rail Mill, where Rose Young worked as a crane operator. The crane can be seen near the top of the photo, from one wall across to the other. It ran along tracks, one along each wall. The crane hook is at the right side. The crane operator sat in a booth behind that hook. Across the centre of the photo are the housings containing the rollers. A red-hot rail is passing through rollers on one of several passes towards forming a rail.

the same length as this room—I could take the straps and put them on the end, lift them over, drop them on the pile, and then take the straps off and come back again. I didn't know that the others couldn't do that, see, 'cause I only worked with Maynard. (*What would the others do?*) Well, they would have to have a crane-chaser take the straps off for them. They would have to follow the crane. They had great big long hooks, and they would unhook the straps off the hot steel. But see, he taught me all this, and I didn't know but what it was part of the job.

He was proud that they'd picked him to break me in in the first place. He was so proud. And he was crazy as the birds, and he and I clicked right from Day One.

Now his son, Roy, was on the other shift. They also later gave him a girl to break in, and of course, the race was on. There was only one job, right? So it was whoever was going to make the best crane-man was going to get the job. There were other cranes for this other girl to get. You know, she wasn't going to be out of a job. But the Rail Mill crane was the piece of cake. So, the race was on. He was determined that I was going to be the one. There seemed to be rivalry.

(*He not only made you a good crane operator, he made you a better one.*) Well, a show-off-y one. I wouldn't say I was better, because I wasn't as fast. I was too careful to take any chances that they would do, for saving time. In other words, both him and Roy would come through the mill, they'd drop their chain on their way in so that the chain was right at the spot. Where I would wait till I got there, and then drop the chain. Because there was too much in between. You know, I wasn't as fast as they were. And I was always scared of hooking the end of the chain into the housing or— you could do a heck of a lot of damage.

I went on the plant on October 19 of '42, and I went over to the Rail Mill the last week of November. And then I was with Maynard—I guess till January, they left me with him to get the training. Perhaps even longer. But then his son, Roy, on the other shift, he went into the army in April—and this is what they were grooming me for. By that time I had taken over the crane.

The interesting part of that is that Maynard became my father-in-law and Roy became my husband. Roy came back in June, and we were married. We met through his father, really. It was unusual. I could see how much like his father he was. And I thought his father—the sun and the stars shone out of his father—he was very, very much like him. (*And they were both crane operators.*) Yes. (*And so were you.*) Yeah.

(*It wasn't enough that you pulled the levers. They wanted you to know the mechanics of the crane as well.*) Nobody wanted me to do it, only Maynard. Now, there was a trouble-man. If there were trouble on different shifts, all we had to do was call a trouble-man. If we had trouble with the electric, we called a fellow from the electric department. And one time a man came up. He said, "I'm from the electric department." And I said, "Okay." "What do you do," he said, "if the fingers on your board jam?" I looked at him and I said, "I change them." He said, "You what?" I said, "I change them." He said, "Show me." He didn't believe me. So I took the skirt off the box, and I took one that was kind of frayed, and I put a new finger on it, and I put the thing back on. He said, "Do you know what you're doing? You're taking my job." He said, "I often wondered how come we don't get a call on your shift." And he said, "Now, I know." He said, "Maynard." They never got any calls off Maynard's shift, but they knew him so long, and they knew that he knew as much about the crane as the fellows that had to come to fix it. And what he knew, he taught me, see. But I never realized that there was a certain man for a certain job. I had never worked under that system before.

(*Would being a crane operator be considered a dangerous job?*) Not in most areas. The only place that I figure would be, would be the Rail Mill and the Open Hearth. Both of those. The Open Hearth has great big pots full of hot lead, and they have to tip that into casts and form blocks. Now, that was a dangerous job. (*How was it dangerous in the Rail Mill?*) Well, you were working so close to the men. Especially when they were changing rolls to make different sizes—the rolls that steel would have to go through to form rails. When they came up, they were just a square block, about 10 by 10. Then they would pass through these, and they'd get smaller. There'd be about three sets. Now, the crane wasn't that far up above the housing. The housings were solid. So the men stood on top of them, and there was an opening that they could go in, to see that the ends of the rolls fitted. So when that turned, as the steel came through the pass, it'd start changing shape. It passed through, and it got skinnier and longer. Then they'd turn, and they'd come through—begin to take shape. They'd get narrow in the centre. You know the way a rail is formed. It's long like that, and then it gets narrow, and then it's flat on the top again. So that would start coming through—it would take another shape. Then it would go back and take another shape. Well, by this time, see, your rail is formed. Now, this is yellow heat. It still had to be hot or they couldn't shape the rails.

(*So you're moving overhead....*) While all this is going on. Now,

I had to lift the rolls, and put the rolls in between those two housings. Those men were all working there. This is why I say it was dangerous. You had to be so careful. And you only had a certain period of time to change the rolls—about four hours, it took me, to change the rolls. Well, perhaps Maynard and Roy could do it in 3½; it would take me almost four hours to change that, a complete change. (*And you're setting up for different widths and thicknesses of steel?*) Yeah, the poundage. See, the 135-pound rails or 150-pound rails or, if it was mine arches, you stripped it right down from the bottom. It was a different set of rolls altogether that went in for mine arches.

It wasn't really till almost a year that I began to realize how responsible the job was. Because the novelty was so different to anything I had ever done. I had been a clerk in a store. And it gradually sank in.

I found men more careless than women, while I was on the plant. They have steps for you to go up, especially in the Plate Mill—you'd go up the steps and then go down, like that. The men wouldn't bother about the steps. They'd jump on the plates with the rollers moving and the plates moving, and they would jump off. You never saw a woman do it. She's too careful of her limbs to take any chances, stupid things that some of the men used to do. Another thing: I used to carry steel on a magnet. Well, a magnet— you can't depend on it any time because it's only on an electric wire. And some of the fellows used to walk underneath that, no matter how much I banged that bell, the smart alecks would run underneath the loads. And if that electricity had ever given way, they'd have been killed. But you never saw a woman. If you rang the bell, a woman stayed where she was supposed to stay till you passed with the load.

I had no trouble. Never. I was just one of the men. There was a Frenchman there—he was foreman on the shift—he had been there for years. He was like Maynard, he was there for about 35 years. He used to give me the signals. And he'd say to me, "Take it up." Well, that meant just touch the lever. And he'd holler, "Blue hair." Well, that meant you just blew on the lever, because that's how much difference it would make in the steel. But he used to swear

and curse at the men all the time. Oh, and he'd get vicious if you took it up a little bit too much, and you'd have to put it back down again. So anyhow, this day, the superintendent came. And he said to me, "How are you two getting along?" I said, "Well, I'll tell you the truth. He curses and swears at me the same as he does the men." "Well," he said, "don't let it worry you, because if he couldn't swear, he couldn't talk." After that, I didn't mind him swearing at me. Half of the time it was in French, I didn't understand it anyway.

(Not only were you well trained, you felt like you were one of the men, you really had a position there. Weren't you angry about losing your job?) Well, I knew it was only temporary, we all knew that when we went to the plant. Only till the boys came back. It was only a temporary measure. *(Did you desire to stay on?)* Well, not really. No, I was willing enough for Roy to come back and for him to do the work. No, I didn't feel bad about it. I went on in October of '42, and it was January of '45. *(No regrets?)* None. I never felt any resentment or anything like that, because we all knew when we went there we were only taking the places of the men till the men came back. And they were starting to come back by then.

(In your heart, though, did anything change about the kind of jobs that women should do?) No. I don't think it's a place for a woman, really. I really don't. It's so dirty. Everybody there, their lungs are full of the smoke and the oil. All that, you get it right in the face all the time when you're working. When my husband died, they did an autopsy on him, and his heart was encrusted. And it was nothing else but all the oil. Of course he used to drink, too, and

he smoked—so between it all.... And Maynard was never without a cough, never. Of course, he used to smoke, too. But all that had to get into your lungs. (*And you feel it was too dirty for a woman?*) Yeah. Well, it's too dirty for a man, too, physically. But it had to be done.

(*So you didn't have regrets when it was over?*) No. Perhaps it was because Roy was going to take back his job, perhaps that was the reason why I had no regrets. I don't know. (*Did you love him already?*) Oh, yeah. He went in April, he went into the army, and he came back in June, and we were married.

(*So you had already kind of got that started before he went into the army.*) That's right. I remember when he went to get the marriage slip. He went to a man to look for the license. And the fellow said to him, "What do you do? What's your occupation?" He said, "I'm a crane-man." He said, "And your bride-to-be?" He said, "Crane-man." He said, "I mean your bride-to-be." "Well," he said, "crane-man." He said, "My God, man, I can't put that on the certificate. I'll have to put 'crane-woman.'" So he put "crane-woman" on the slip. We used to laugh about that.

CHAPTER 8

Work Poetry of John J. "Slim" MacInnis

by Don MacGillivray

A few days after "Doscomocracy" was published in the *Steelworker & Miner* on 9 January 1943, Sydney steelworkers went on strike. They were joined by others in Trenton, Nova Scotia, and Sault Ste. Marie, Ontario. It was not a complete surprise to anyone; a strike vote a few months earlier in the "Steel City" had resulted in a 3,074 to 38 count in favour of such action. The issues were many and included opposition to wage controls and a desire for a fair wage—Sydney steelworkers, at 45 cents/hour, were far removed from the 78 cents/hour paid to their American counterparts. They were recently organized and, as "Doscomocracy" suggests, were determined to improve their condition in the expanding war economy.

"Doscomocracy"

My back is bent from a lifetime spent
In the dirt and steam and snow—
In the General Yard, where the work is hard
And the wages mean and low.

My hands are swelled from the spades I've held
In the depths of a dirty ditch
And my shoulders sprung from the picks I've swung
In the toils of the idle rich.

My eyes are dimmed from the years spent in
The glare of the Open Hearth
And my lungs are shot from gasses caught
In DOSCO's hell on earth.

My heart is strained and my legs are sprained
And a din roars in my ears
From toiling in moulds and greasy holes
That has shortened my life by years.

And many a time I came out to find
That I'd only come out on spec.
When jobs were few and old Bruno's crew
Were all old Peter checked.[1]

For times get hard in the General Yard
When steel goes in a slump
And Saunders' friends are thankful then
For the checkers and the dump.[2]

While my hair has greyed I've begged and prayed
For a job I might enjoy
But I leaned on luck while the plumbs were plucked
By the bosses' fair haired boy.

Then the war came on and my boy has gone
And his mother's heart must fret.
Who pays the tax on the gun he packs
While they're working his Dad to death.

Now my health is ruined and I'll soon be doomed
To a cold dark debtor's grave
Is a few cents raise in my last few days
Too much for a lifetime slave?
                                        —Pro Bono Proletariat

John J. "Slim" MacInnis had been back working at the Steel
Plant in Sydney for about three years when he wrote
"Doscomocracy." It was the first of a small number of verses com-

---

[1] Bruno was an Italian cement worker brought in during the 1923 strike; Peter
was a general foreman in the General Yard. John J. "Slim" MacInnis: "Every Sunday Peter had a chicken that the Ukrainians brought out to him, and they kept him
in cigars. That was the time they all paid for their jobs."
[2] Saunders was a superintendent in the General Yard. The checkers were a
latticework of brick under the stacks in the Open Hearth. They had to be replaced
often. Both the checkers and the slag dumps were always a source of work.

posed over a 50-year period dealing with and coming directly from
the experiences of a Sydney steelworker. Whatever their literary
qualities, they read well and a couple of them have become relatively
well known within the working
class of industrial Cape Breton.
Two at least were retyped and cir-
culated—anonymously—for
years; one was read out at a labour
rally in the Steelworker's Hall in
Sydney some years ago. Recently
they surfaced again.

John J. "Slim" MacInnis

Slim MacInnis' literary output
was not large. But his industrial
verse captured the attitudes, practices, experiences and feelings of
two generations of steelworkers in Sydney. His sparse output and
his inclination to use pseudonyms ensured a lack of recognition.
He was a reserved individual although many workers knew him
and some of them were aware of his literary bent. Only on a couple
of occasions however were his contributions along this line directly
linked to him. Yet they continued to circulate and to be appreciated. One suspects this is at least partly due to the scarcity of steelworkers' songs and verse in the area. Mind, there is that second
verse of "The DOSCO Boys"—to the air of the "Notre Dame
March" no less—which is contained in a song sheet put out by the
Industrial Relations Department of DOSCO in the 1950s:

> We are the boys who roll out the steel
> Give 'em the stuff with lots of appeal
> We make billets, bars and rails
> The coke, the wire and the rails.
> After we get the coal and the ore
> Begins the rest of all our chores
> DOMCOs, DISCOs, DOSCOs too
> I'd bet you'd like to join us too.

145

Views from the Steel Plant

Tripe aside, there seem to be only jocular albeit not inaccurate ones such as "Dumping Slag over to the Steel Plant," which describes the initial impressions of someone coming to live and attempting to sleep in close proximity to the plant, or more recent plaintive, quasi-militant ones like "Let's Save Our Industry" from the 1960s. ["It brought us joy and brought us tears/ It's been here over sixty years/ It built our homes and stilled our fears/ And made this island what it is./ *Chorus:* Let's save our industry.../ The industry we need..." by Charlie MacKinnon. See page 185.] Few have come from within the plant gates. The substantial amount of verse and song which came out of the working class struggles of industrial Cape Breton—one thinks espe-cially of the writings of Dawn Fraser, and pieces such as "Arise Ye Nova Scotia Slaves" and "The Yahie Miners"—have concentrated lit-tle on the situation of the Sydney steelworkers.

Yet the strength of local traditions in industrial Cape Breton, the richness of the sources from which it draws, has been recog-nized.[1] A recent article makes it clear that the "country of coal" is well represented.[2] The same cannot be said of the steelmaking por-tion of the industry. Even Dawn Fraser makes only fleeting refer-ence in his work [*Echoes from Labor's Wars*], mentioning the pro-vincial police charge on churchgoers in 1923 in an ode to Forman Waye, a steelworker leader of the 1920s.[3] MacInnis is himself una-ware of other steelworkers using the pen as an industrial weapon.

"Slim" MacInnis was born in the Ashby area of Sydney in 1911. At eighteen he started at the Steel Plant. Six months later, in October 1929, he was laid off. That winter he managed two more

---

[1] David Frank, "Tradition and Culture in the Cape Breton Mining Community in the Early Twentieth Century," in K. Donovan, ed., *Cape Breton at 200* (Sydney 1985), 203-18; Charles W. Dunn, *Highland Settler: A Portrait of the Scottish Gael in Cape Breton and Eastern Nova Scotia* (Breton Books, 1991).

[2] An excellent introduction to this still neglected area is David Frank, "The Industrial Folk Song in Cape Breton," *Canadian Folklore Canadien*, 8, 1-2 (1986) 21-42. See also Helen Creighton and Calum MacLeod, *Gaelic Songs in Nova Scotia* (Ottawa 1979); John C. O'Donnell, *The Men of the Deeps* (Waterloo 1975); Ron MacEachern, ed., *Songs and Stories from Deep Cove, Cape Breton* (Sydney 1979); Alphonse MacDonald, *Cape Breton Songster* (n.p. 1935); Stuart McCawley, *Cape Breton Come-All-Ye* (Glace Bay 1966 [1929]).

[3] *Echoes from Labor's Wars—The Expanded Edition* by Dawn Fraser, Breton Books (1992).

146

months on the plant but after a 30-day period without a shift, "I threw my lunch can and cheque number away and gave it up." Like many single, young men he "rode the rods" for much of the next decade. It was "the most interesting period of my life...." (During that period he did work for close to a year on the "Black Diamond" boats carrying coal and rails.)

Ten years later he returned, initially working for a contractor dismantling Number 8 Blast Furnace. When the job was completed he again joined the DOSCO work force. He had not forgotten the lost decade and his first attempt at writing verse occurred in this transitional period from the Depression to the war economy. It was published by M. A. MacKenzie in the *Steelworker & Miner* and immediately subjected to the scrutiny of government officials. They were not amused.

From Breadlines to Battlefields

For years in vain we fought to gain,
We of the workless mass,
A chance to work though our struggle irked
The idle and wealthy class.

Deprived of a home we were forced to roam,
A hungry and ragged throng.
And few were the friends
    we encountered then
To lighten our way along.

Though mill and mine of every kind
With idle goods were stacked,
And vaults were stored with a golden hoard
Still we of the workless lacked.

Nor statesmen cared at the way we fared,
Though poverty seared our souls.
We had only the jail and the hungry trail
To a flophouse dark and cold.

While pompous priests,
    from their pulpits screeched
Of heaven and love and truth.
We lived in a hell and learned too well
The curse of a squandered youth.

They paid scant heed to our grievous need,
Though pledged to uphold His word.
They shared the best and they cared the less
For the sheep of the common herd.

In vain we fought to improve our lot
But our rights they refused to give.
Though all we asked was an honest task
That would make life fit to live.

But never a cent could be had or spent—
No "hunger fund" was raised.
The workless class—we were only trash,
Unworthy of help or praise.

But today in fear as danger is near,
From a source they helped to build,
They look to us when they find they must
And our blood would ask us spill.

What right, we ask, have this useless class
To demand we engage a foe
They helped maintain with the selfish aim
Of saving the "status quo"?

Why should we band in a far-off land
And wealth for another wrest,
If here at home we have only known
The fate of the dispossessed?

What's left to lose if we should refuse
To fight for De-mockery?
In the name of Christ what a costly price
They should ask for our poverty.
    —Beachcomber
Steelworker & Miner, 17 August 1940

John J. MacInnis: "And they were out asking me to be a sucker to go out and get shot—Christ—for $30 a month. Imagine....
"The country was always in turmoil around those times. George MacEachern and a few more that were in the Party...I remember down at the Lyceum they wanted an open forum—and they wanted the government to show their confidence in Canada by taking two billion dollars and putting on a big program of public works. Of course, 'Where's the money coming from?' was always the story. But the day the goddamn war started, two billion went over as credit to Britain."

Inspired, enthused, or just content to get the phrases out of his head and down on paper, MacInnis immediately wrote two more: "I don't know if you call it writing or not, but that's just a source of annoyance to me now because a phrase will pop into my mind and then I feel I got to put it into a rhyme or some damn thing or another. That's pretty well how they started." (Family tradition has his grandfather, also John, as a writer of songs and verse.)

These initial efforts were, however, thwarted. As the editor of the *Steelworker & Miner* soon explained on the front page (in) "A Word to 'Beachcomber': We are forced to inform 'Beachcomber,' the local poet, that we cannot publish his two last contributions because we have been officially informed that his poem 'From Breadlines to Battlefields,' which we published the week before last, contravenes the 'Defence of Canada Regulations.'

"We have reason to believe that certain potential fascists holding high positions, whom we have occasion to castigate from time to time are constantly 'drawing the attention' of the authorities to items in the 'Steelworker and Miner' which are not to their fascist tastes. Our readers can guess who they are."

MacInnis was little concerned about the attention and he continued to write, although only his "romantic" verse made it into the newspapers for the next couple of years. (John MacInnis: "M. A. MacKenzie was informed from Ottawa that if he printed any more of that 'tripe' as they called it that they'd shut him up. It didn't bother me.")

Early in 1943 he began his industrial verse with "Doscomocracy." He followed this up with his most popular work, "DOSCO's Inferno," a personalized account of work in the Open Hearth department.

148

DOSCO's Inferno

Oh! tired am I of the ceaseless toil
And the endless cares and woes
Of the paupered years
    and the deathless fears
That a low paid worker knows.

All my toil filled life
    has been fraught with strife
And all that I have to show
Are the callused palms
    of these workworn hands
And a faltering step and slow.

From my early youth like a soul-less brute
In a Godless way I've slaved,
In DOSCO's mills where the labour kills
And hastens an early grave.

I've shovelled ore thru a furnace door
In the heat of the boiling steel
Where the stink and glare
    of the poisoned air
Makes a man feel faint and reel.

Oh! I've grown sick of the look of brick
And the paddles and tongs and pails
Of the mud and the mire and McIntyre
And the flame that never fails.

The checkers so hot and Foreman Watt
And Ritchie who's always there
Like a Simon Legree he seems to me
With a cruel and crafty stare.

The charging cars and the hammer and bars
And the smoke of the metal trains

The ladles and pans, the barrow and fans
And the screech of the hoisting cranes.

Oh! weary am I of the few who try
To scab and pamper the boss
Confidential men and those who pretend
A concern for production lost.

For the many must work
    for the few who shirk
The high paid few who prize
The money and ease and the luxuries
Of private enterprise.

Those hypocrites who rack their wits
And worry and scheme and plan
For a christian way to lower the pay
Of the honest working man.

But bear in mind there will come a time
And come it soon, I pray
When the stooge and boss aside we'll toss
And build for a better day.

Then we'll produce for the common use
For the man in field and ditch,
And we'll liquidate the profit rate
Along with the idle rich.

So for better or worse I'll end this verse
On a note of hope my friend
"There's a crimson star that shines afar,
And the longest night must end."

—Little Twisted
Steelworker & Miner
13 October 1945

"DOSCO's Inferno" was an immediate hit at the plant. According to the author: "The only one that ever got any kind of recognition was that Open Hearth one. I was pointed out by nearly every god-damn guy in the mill. 'That's the guy that wrote it, that's the guy.' Ritchie was talking to Watt one day: 'That's him over there,' you know, that sort of stuff. That went all through the mill. Didn't bother me." It continues to circulate.

John J. MacInnis: "I was a committee man in the Plate Mill during the war there in fact.... I carried on a class struggle locally for all my life. If anyone ever said anything about Russia, I always thought I should be there to defend it. So anyhow I got blamed for being the agitator on the Grievance Committee. The Super told somebody they were having a lot of trouble with the union. I think they were referring to me. There were about 200 people all around my age, maybe a little older, some of the rollers. And we all got deferred from the Army because we were in essential industry, as they called it.

"And the first thing I know I get a goddamn draft notice in the mail. And I was naive enough to think...well, that was just the way they do business. Like it was in a pile and they picked it out. And what it was, the goddamn Super wanted to get rid of me. So he got the Army to call me up. Well, the Army turned me down. I spent nearly a month in Halifax before I got out of the bloody thing. And when I came back and told him that I'd be back to work next week— such a look came over his face, it paid for all the trouble it caused me."

The following months were turbulent ones in the Canadian steel industry. There were several walkouts at the Sydney plant in early 1946 and they culminated in a general walkout on 15 July. Slim immediately wrote "The Steel Strike."

The Steel Strike

If you'll listen friend for a moment then
A brief account I'll give
Of a worker's woe when the rates are low
And the struggle it is to live.

Sure the plant's on strike,
    you can say what you like
Or think what you like as well;
But for years we've tried for a raise denied
While DOSCO's profits swelled.

We played the game and were not to blame,
We pleaded from board to board,
But never a cent for the sweat we spent
Would they give from their greedy hoard.

I live in a shack but the rent fell back
And the landlord threatened then
That he'd get rid of my wife and kid
While I was at work, my friend.

So each day in the mill, my heart was filled
With a dread that was always hell;
For the law was strict and they might evict
The ones I loved so well.

How I've lain awake
    and my heart has ached

Through many a lonely night,
And I cursed and swore as I paced the floor
With no relief in sight.

Oh: I prayed to the saints in heaven, friend,
And I cursed to the IMPS in hell
Till my nerves were frayed, but it didn't aid
The hurt in my heart that swelled.

No hope could I see in my misery
But only a life of want,
Tho' I scrimped and saved,
    and I toiled and saved
Until I grew thin and gaunt.

How we pleaded in vain again and again
While the cost of living soared,
On our failing rate we lost all faith
In government labor boards.

But at last there came an end to the pain
And my heart no more could feel,
Then the talks were stalled
    and the union called
For a national strike in steel.

So we're struck at last and all we ask
Is a forty hour week

150

So our brave young sons
    who fought the huns
Can find the work they seek.

And a slight increase that will give release
From the worry we long have known,
And a chance to pay for the right to stay
In the hovel we call our home.

That's our well-won right
    and we're proud to fight

Till we all lie dead or jailed,
For we just can't live on the wage they give—
We've tried for years and failed.

So now my friend my tale I'll end,
Well, we know our cause is just,
And God pity the scab that our pickets grab
Who tries to betray our trust.

—Slim
Steelworker & Miner, 27 July 1946

The Sydney steelworkers finally went back to work in October. The decline of the steel and coal industry in Cape Breton continued.

In 1970 as Slim MacInnis was preparing to retire after more than 30 years at the plant he wrote "Steelworker's Lament." He was 59. Most of that time he had operated out of the General Yard and, as his verse suggests, had worked throughout the plant during those decades. DOSCO had disappeared in 1967 and the Sydney plant was now operated by the Nova Scotia government (Sydney Steel Corporation/SYSCO). The legacy, the costs, were still being added up. Perhaps this continuity is one of the reasons why "Steelworker's Lament" also continues to circulate.

Steelworker's Lament

I've worked on the steel plant all my life
Since the time I was just a lad,
The hours were long
    but my back was strong
And I gave them all I had.

I've shovelled their snow at ten below
From tracks piled high and white
While the city dozed I worked and froze
There many a winter night.

I've shovelled their coal to a boiler old
And just as hot as the grates of hell,
Just useless trash most stone and ash
That the coal mines couldn't sell.

I've loaded their rails and packed their nails
And bundled their rods and bars,
And I've gasped and choked
    in the poison smoke
And the fumes of their hot coke cars.

I've swung a sledge on the crumbling edge
Of a furnace wide and tall
With my vision blurred with the dust it stirred
And a man just dared not fall.

I've shovelled their ore
    from the stinking floor
Of Ships from beyond the seas,
And my stomach turned
    with the gas was churned
From shovelling manganese.

I've burned my feet in the hellish heat
Of a slag-pit's fiery glow,
And I've froze my ears
    at the scrap yard shears
On a night that was ten below.

I've swabbed their sewers
    where a man endures
A stench that's beyond compare,

Views from the Steel Plant

In air so foul that the rodents who prowl
Have all abandoned there.

Now my nerves are frayed
    and my hair has greyed
And slowed are my work-worn hands,
And my back is bent
    from the youth I've spent
At Sydney Steel's demands.

For a man that toils in a steel mill spoils
His chance for a ripe old age

For the hazards to health are early felt
And he's old at middle age.

Now these are but few of the jobs I do
That briefly I've made mention
And I feel in my heart
    that I've played my part,
And I've earned an early pension.

—in the *Highlander*
Sydney, 19 August 1970

Slim MacInnis' last published work appeared in a local newspaper in 1988, 44 years after his initial, upsetting-to-some, "From Breadlines to Battlefields." The verse, "Tramping Down the Highway" [fragment from *The Northside Tribune*, North Sydney, 10 August 1988], is a comment on the contemporary conditions now prevalent in the industrial Cape Breton area.

When you've used up all your pogey
And can't pay your room and board
And you're tramping down the highway
Dreaming dreams you can't afford....

And the whole darn Constitution
Wouldn't buy a single meal
When you're tramping down the highway
Or laid-off at Sydney Steel....

Not much had altered in 60 years. The workforce at the plant is now settling at a little over 700 [as of 1991] and the out-migration has increased. In his writings Slim MacInnis had come full circle. He has also left a small but valuable record of impressions and comments in verse of working at the Steel Plant in Sydney.

John J. MacInnis: "I had no use for school at all. Not a bit. When I was about twelve my old man decided he was going to move out to Grand Lake.... That would be considered pioneering today because of the way we lived. Got our water from a spring, chop wood for heat, no phone, no electric light, nothing.

"Lived out there for four years and then we moved back to Sydney. School about 400 to 500 feet away at Grand Lake. We went up to Grade 8 there and then I had to go to the Academy. So I spent two years at the Academy and I didn't get a good pass mark because I didn't know a goddamn thing about algebra. It was a foreign language as far as I was concerned. We didn't have it in the country school. But they had it in the city schools so they were a whole year ahead of me on that. I could never catch up. So I gave it up, I quit, and went to work at the Steel Plant."

John J. "Slim" MacInnis (photo by Don MacGillivray)

CHAPTER 9

C. M. (Clem) Anson— A Life in Steel

My father was in steelmaking. And my grandfather. My grandfather went over in the States with Carnegie at one time, building blast furnaces for him. And he built one of the first blast furnaces in India, about 1901, just about the time I was born. And my great-grandfather had his own little shop in the backyard of his house, where he made knives outside Sheffield.

I started in 1915, in Australia. My father was manager of the only steel plant in Australia, when he went up in 1910 or something like that. They took him out of England to start up the first electric steelmaking furnace in Australia, a small one. Not too long after that he took me out of school and put me in the lab. I used to do the steel analysis, by following the book. Test to get the right carbon content. So I wasn't quite 15 when I first went to work in a steel plant.

(*And at 14, your life's direction was pretty well set.*) Oh it was, definitely. I always loved it. I used to go with my dad on Sundays when I was a little shaver, Sunday morning—6 years old. I've always known what I wanted to be. Oh I was lucky in that respect. I wanted to be a steelmaker. I worked with my father in Australia. He stayed with that new plant a little more than a year—then he went back to his old plant in Australia. And I started working in the rolling mills there. I was more of a chaser for the boss, messenger. I was only 15 years old.

Then I went to the Open Hearth and started working on the furnaces. Third Helper. I was doing a man's job, that's all. Third Helper—that's the lowest in the furnace crew at the Open Hearth. I shoveled limestone, iron ore, anything that had to be shoveled. Wielded the sledge. In those days we didn't have the type of furnace you see here, where they tilt. It was stationary furnace with a tap hole in them, and when a heat was ready you had to drive a bar through a tapping hole at the back of the furnace—inch, inch-and-a-quarter bar—and you drove that with a 12- or 14-pound sledge until you drove that through, and the molten metal would come out. Oh yes, it was a long time before I needed a desk at a steel plant.

The First World War was on and First and Second Helpers were leaving the plant to enlist—so I got promoted fairly fast. Within a year I was First Helper, with very little experience. I was there a little over two years. Then the second electric plant was built in Australia, and the man who was going to boss that plant offered me a job, and I moved there on my 18th birthday, to be assistant to the guy they were bringing out from the States to start up the plant. Within three or four months they sent him back and they gave me his job. Only 18 years old. And I ran the electric furnace part of that plant for nearly two years. I was doing a man's job. I looked more than 18—and I had some experience.

Then my dad came to visit me. Took me to the hotel for dinner. Asked me, "How much notice do you have to give them to leave?" I thought he was crazy. Here I was boss of my end of the plant. The world was already my oyster and I had it well-opened. I was drawing big money—about $52 a month in those days. He said, "I want you to go back to school." Said, "You haven't got enough education to get where you want to go in this world, I hope." And the upshot was, I gave my resignation the next morning. Within a month I landed in Montreal and went up to McGill to get in. I studied metallurgy and engineering—the science faculty, it was called—graduated in spring of 1925.

(*Did you know about Sydney Steel?*) Not a thing. (*They weren't discussing it in the classrooms at McGill?*) No. But I wanted to work in Canada and the States for a while before I went home. It was a bad time for steelmaking with Depression on. But they had a new man here [in Sydney], a general manager, his name was Kelly— H. J. Kelly. They brought him from Lackawanna [New York] in 1924 to head up this steel plant at Sydney. He was at McGill, saw the head of the metallurgical department, told them he was looking for a young man to come down to Sydney to be trained—and I happened to go in a couple days later. I don't remember what for. "Oh," he said, "I thought of you a few days ago. But I knew you had a job, so I didn't bother you."

Jeez, that's what I'd been looking for. He gave me the address. I wrote them, gave my resumé. Had a letter back; Kelly said he'd be in Montreal in a couple, three weeks' time. Then I hardly got that letter before I got another one from him. "Don't bother waiting. Job here if you want it. Want somebody in our Blast Furnace department. Will pay $125 a month." Peanuts. "Come, and the job's yours." I left that night on the train. Labourer's wages were 27 cents an hour, about three dollars a day if you worked 12 hours—I guess I wasn't quite getting labourer's wage!

I came. They put me through the plant. I started at the Open Hearth. Worked in that for a couple of months. (*Supervising?*) Oh, hell no. Labourer. And up at the Coke Ovens. I was there for six or eight weeks. I wasn't supervising. I was just a learning young fellow. And then took me down the Blast Furnace—this is where they were aiming me for—the old man who was superintendent of Blast Furnaces was then over 60, and they wanted somebody to fill in when he got out. But turned out he had no intention of getting out. So I'm working on the Blast Furnace, still labouring. Oh, I was at that for about a year, I guess—and getting to a point where I was about getting fed up. Thought perhaps I'd better get out unless I could see something different.

So one day I stopped the boss, this fellow Kelly, when he came through the plant one Sunday morning. He asked me how things

were going around the Blast Furnaces. I asked him, "How'm I doing, Mr. Kelly?" Said, "You haven't heard any complaints from
me, have you?"—that's the kind of guy he was. "No, I'd just like to
know." "All right." "Then how about giving me a raise." The end
of the month my pay cheque came down—$150. I called him up
on the phone. "I got my cheque, Mr. Kelly." "Oh, wonderful, Clem."
I said, "Wonderful.... I'm through!" I can see the head clerk in the
Blast Furnace office. Wouldn't believe anybody would talk to Mr.
Kelly, the general manager, in that fashion. He quieted me down
finally, said he'd have another look. So next month—$175. Well,
that was getting on to something half decent. Made me superintendent of the Blast Furnaces, of the whole Blast Furnace department.

(*What would other labourers say to this promotion?*) Well,
there was no one working on the Blast Furnaces with the compe-
tency to be the assistant superintendent. (*And no union at that time.*)
No union. Anyhow, then they started up a new department in the
Rolling Mills, making the high-carbon plates that go underneath
the rails on every tie—they put me in charge.

In 1928, they made me assistant general superintendent of the
whole plant, and I was only 27 years old. This was fantastic. (*Do
you think they made a mistake?*) No, no. And a year and a half after
that, I was made assistant general manager for the whole business—
BESCO, as it was called then.

(*Why did they put so much on you?*) Well, they didn't have any
skilled technical personnel. Everybody there except the general
manager had grown up either there or some other place around
Nova Scotia—trained to be a mechanic, for instance, started in the
Rolling Mills and gradually came to be a roller—the top job in the
Rolling Mill other than the supervisory staff. In those days, it wasn't
anything like it got to be later on, that you took college-trained
people and trained them. You worked at the work and gradually
got promoted and perhaps became a foreman, and went from there
to be something else.

(*Is it true that Kelly kind of picked you out and helped you up
the ladder a little quicker than a person could go today?*) Yes.
Number One, I was a graduate metallurgist. Number Two, I was

taller than he was—he was short. That's important to some people's thinking. If you're short, sometimes you've got a thing about life, you know? He had a graduate metallurgist already *here*. A local boy. Shorter than he was. And then I think what really started him—I talked back to him.

Kelly was a good manager. He hadn't been to college. He'd come up through the ranks. But got to be boss of the rolling mills in Lackawanna, superintendent of all their rolling mills. And the people in Sydney, looking for somebody who knew something about steel to take over, hired him to come down here and made him general manager. Kelly was a steelmaker. But he knew very little about blast furnaces. But he was a good operator—and a good millman. I doubt that you'd find even today a steel mill where the general manager had any experience in every department. I was kind of lucky that way.

(*The people who actually owned the plant, were they steelmakers themselves?*) Oh, no. One owned big clothing stores in Montreal. (*So what were they if they weren't steelmakers?*) Well, what would you call them? Entrepreneurs? Or something of that nature. A fellow called Roy Wolvin. When I came here he was president of the company that owned this place and a few others— British Empire Steel Corporation. (*And what did he know about how to make steel?*) Not a bloody thing. Not one thing. That's why he got a man like Kelly to come here, somebody who *did* know something. (*So their skill is in finding men who can make steel.*) Right. And finding how best to operate. They saw an opportunity here. In the old days it was the raw material—the proximity of coal and iron ore within 350 miles. (*And Sydney Harbour?*) Well, yes, a good harbour. But iron and coal are the two main ingredients of steel. If you haven't got them, you can't make steel.

(*What did you find here in the way of a steel plant when you came to Cape Breton?*) An old plant, 25 years old. It wasn't a good plant. The Open Hearth was a very poor arrangement. As far as I know, it was the only open hearth ever built that way. It had ten 50-ton furnaces. And the working platform, the charging platform, as it's called, of the Open Hearth, was at ground level—you won't find that anywhere. You will never see that again. (*Why?*) Else-

where, it's always up in the air so that the underside of the furnace—the checker chambers and all that—so *they* can be above
ground. Here in Sydney, the checkers were underground. Consequently, when you had to change the checkers, which you did every
few months, you had to take the floor up, and then take the top off
the checker chamber—and then go down and throw out the old
bricks and lay new bricks in their place. And there were four of
these to every furnace. Consequently, it interfered with the charging machine's going back and forth. That's the way the plant was
built in the first place. I don't know what crazy idea the guy had. It
was the worst idea ever promulgated for a steel plant, for an open
hearth.

(*Some people have said that when Sydney Steel was built, it
was the state of the art, that it was the finest at that time.*) That's
just not true. This open hearth plan, for instance—that's the worst
thing they could have done. Had to take it up every few months,
from underground, for every furnace—and there were 10 furnaces
in a line. Those checkers were an error. Costly in terms of money
as well as time. And they operated [like that] all through the Second World War. And that was just one of many things we needed to
do to improve the plant.

The only trouble that made it somewhat slow was that we didn't
have the money. And in those days the government wouldn't give
you any money. And nobody else would. You had to earn the money
before you could spend it on improving the plant. In 1926, we were
broke. We were in receivership—the courts put it there—it couldn't
pay its bills. It hadn't been making money, I guess, not since the
First World War. And whatever money they made in the First World
War, they took out of it, they didn't put it back in the plant. (*The
owners did?*) Yeah. (*They didn't invest in rebuilding the plant after
the war?*) No. It would have been wise, but they didn't do it. (*The
plant made profit during the war.*) Every steel plant made profits.
(*And when you came here, you saw no evidence that they had taken
those profits and plowed it back into the business?*) Just the opposite. You knew they hadn't. You could see that they hadn't. A lot of
the equipment was getting out of date.

But this man Kelly, he took ahold. We put a proposition up to the board of directors every year which added up to a few million dollars, very few. I think the highest proposition I ever put to them was about 10 million for a year's spending on capital expenditures—though 10 million those days was a lot more than 10 million today. We would look at the whole plant and say, what is the most important thing to do, what should be done first?—because a lot of things would pay off if you did them. What's the best? Should we do something at the Blast Furnace this year? May do something at the Open Hearth next year. Or may do something at both one year. Rolling Mills. Blooming, Billet Mill, Rail Mills, Bar Mills, Rod Mill—and then the Wire and Nail Mill.

You would have to assess the situation as to how much money *might* be available from profits you'd make—have to be mostly profits—wasn't anybody investing money in the plant in those days. One year after another, you'd improve the plant, whatever money

In the Number 1 Open Hearth Shop (1901-1950), the charging car moves through pouring molten iron into one of the 10-ton furnaces. The furnaces were at floor level and the checkers were under that floor. For fifty years, those checkers had to be dug up and repaired, as Clem Anson describes.

was available. As long as I was over there we did that. And we built it up to a damned efficient little steel plant.

(*Was it in good shape before the Second World War? Did you have it built up by then?*) No, it wasn't. For instance, we hadn't got the mill electrified in the Second World War. We were still using those bloody old 50-ton furnaces down on the ground in the Open Hearth—they operated all through the Second War. And going into the war, we still had only the same two raw materials and the size of the plant first—it was only a 500,000-ton plant. And we kept it busy all the time. But the type of plant it was, and those raw materials, didn't stop us making good steel. Nobody made better than we did, as a matter of fact.

And as for rails, we made the best rails in the world—no question about that.

And all rails made in the world today are made according to the process we developed right here: the Mackie Retarded Cooling Process—either that or something that came out of it.

We had a tremendous reputation on rails. We shipped them all over. India. South Africa, several countries in South America. And of course, CN and CP [Canadian National and Canadian Pacific railroads]. (*Would rails alone be enough to carry that plant and make it profitable?*) No, we couldn't get enough rail business. I think about the highest production in rail we ever got to in my time was—well, we might have hit 200,000 tons in a year, but I don't think quite—but that wouldn't be enough. You needed twice that much.

But we were shipping to England steel in various forms. Billets, for instance, went out of here by the cargo load—10,000 to 12,000 tons at a time—send them over. Rods. Thousand and thousands of tons of those we shipped to England. All kind of qualities. Made high-grade wire or soft wire or anything—whatever they wanted, we made it. We had an awfully good reputation in England for the quality of our steel. And we made money then. I think the first steel we shipped over to England would be in 1932—not long after we came out of receivership.

(*In other words, the whole world goes into Depression, and the Steel Plant at Sydney is able to come out of receivership?*) We were out of the Depression long before the rest of the steel industry in this continent was out of it—because we went into export. That's one reason why. And the other big thing, we developed the Mackie Retarded Cooling Process. When we came out of receivership, a new company was formed—Dominion Steel and Coal Corporation [DOSCO]. It owned this plant and it owned the plants in Trenton and the Halifax Shipyards, plus a small nail-making plant in Saint John, New Brunswick, and a small rolling mill in Montreal, the Peck Rolling Mill—and, of course, they owned the coal company. When these people formed DOSCO, they put in a retired insurance man as president for a while—he didn't last very long, wasn't meant to. Then came Sir Newton Moore. And he was the one who thought we should export steel to England—beyond the rails we were already exporting. And the first thing I think we shipped there was nails—hundredweight bags of nails—112 pounds. We wouldn't ship them in just by the carload. We'd have several hundred tons on a vessel. Build it up and build it up. Then started the rods going over there. England imported from the continent several million tons of steel a year in various forms. And we were able to compete.

You see, we had an exceptional overall work force, particularly in the supervisory group—heads of departments, foremen of groups—we couldn't have done all that we did without that. Because we didn't have good raw materials to work with. Our iron ore was one of the poorest iron ores to smelt in the world, a very dense hematite. And contained an awful lot of silicon—perhaps 15 per cent. And unfortunately contained a lot of phosphorus, which you don't want in steel too much. And there weren't too many places in those days you could get iron ore. Iron ore wasn't as plentiful then as it is today—at least it hadn't been discovered. In fact, there was no iron ore mined in Canada—and Newfoundland was not Canada in those days—east of a small deposit in Ontario. And there was none mined west of that. All the iron ore for central Canadian plants—ALGOMA, STELCO, DOFASCO—came from the Mesabi iron ore range in Pennsylvania. All of our ore came from Newfoundland. All of our Blast Furnace ore. And it was very poor. It was about 50 per cent iron, which wasn't bad—nothing wrong with that. And 15 per cent silicon meant you had to put a lot of limestone in the Blast Furnace to take the silicon away as slag—and then all the phosphorus went into the iron and you had to take that out in the Open Hearth. So this was an expensive proposition.

And the same thing about the coal. You know, the Cape Breton coal is not good metallurgical coal. There were a couple of mines that delivered a coal that one could use—but they did not make good coke. Made very weak coke. Weak in strength. And the result was that when it got in the Blast Furnace it broke up before it had done its work. And you had to use more coke than you should have—consequently costing more money. Now we eventually got a way around that by importing a certain amount of low volatile coal from Pennsylvania, about 20 per cent of what we used—and the combination with the high volatile Cape Breton coal made a good coke. So we got our coke consumption down in the Blast Furnace.

There was no steel plant in the world had a poorer ore to make steel from. And the coal was not a good metallurgical coal. (*Wasn't that realized when they were building the plant?*) I don't think so, no.

(*When we talk of why the steel plant first came to Cape Breton, they say we had the coal, we had the iron ore close at hand—what more could you ask for?*) That's right. But I think perhaps you should put it another way. As I told you, there were not too many iron ore deposits discovered in the world, so you made do with whatever you had. And similarly, how many coal deposits are there available to make coke from?... So it *was* a question that coal was here, iron ore was nearby—okay, we can make steel here. And they did.

And freight rates in Canada. We had to compete with plants in central Canada—we had to sell up there at the same price that they charged up there. Nobody would give us more, just because we had to pay to transport the steel a thousand miles to them. We just had to accept whatever price was available up there. So all that meant was per ton of steel produced, we got a little less money than people producing steel in Ontario. They were closer to the market than we were. Of course [at first], we had no market up there. That is to say, we had no *assured* market in the 1920s and early '30s. In fact, it was not until DOSCO was formed that we established subsidiary companies in that area—Quebec and Ontario. We established there because that's where most of the Canadian finished steel was consumed. In order to assure ourselves of the market, we had to establish those subsidiaries....

We sent steel in various types of finish—not completely finished. Wire rods, for instance, from which come nails and all kinds of wire and barbed-wire fences and industrial fencing. Here in Sydney we would roll the steel into something, maybe billets, if it was going to a rolling mill up there for rolling into bars. Or we'd roll it right down to a rod here and ship it to one of these nail-producing plants which we had in Windsor, Toronto, Montreal. In other words, we had an assured market for a reasonable production here.

But we [also] finished and shipped out of here thousands and thousands of tons of nails and fencing wire and barbed wire and all that sort of thing—out around through the Panama Canal up to Vancouver—brought it all the way across from Vancouver to mid-Canada. (*Finished products from Sydney?*) Yes. Finished products from the Sydney Wire Mill. Or in the summertime we'd ship it by lakeboat up the St. Lawrence and through the Canal and into the Lakes as far as Port Arthur—then ship it from there to our customers across the prairie.

We had built up the plant. Modernized it in many respects. For instance, up to about 1937, the biggest steelmaking furnace we had was a 50-tonner—50 English tons, so that was 55 metric tons. We had a couple of duplex furnaces—they were 100-ton furnaces—but they could not produce steel of themselves. You'd take the heat along so far and then tap out 50 tons of it and cart it into the old shop and put it into a 50-ton furnace, finish it off there. Those duplex furnaces had been installed in 1910 or 1912. And we converted them in 1937 or thereabouts to 100-ton self-contained furnaces, so they could make their own steel and finish it, pour it in the building. And just before the war, we completed an addition to that shop and put in two more 100-ton furnaces, so we had four when the war broke out. And not long after the war broke out, we built a fifth furnace. And after the war we built Number 6—but when we built the later furnaces, we made them capable of being expanded easily and made into 225-ton furnaces. Well, that's one

way you build up production: you get greater production per man—
because the work force operating a 50-ton furnace is exactly the
same as the one operating a 250-ton furnace. You made more steel
per hour, using not any more men than the small furnace took.

I told you about the old 50-ton furnaces being down on the
ground. The new shop, Number 2 shop, was all built up in the air,
nothing on the ground, nothing underground—and that made it
easier to make repairs to them. Consequently, you used less labour
in making the repairs.

(*So this is an example of capital investment that paid off by in-
creasing your production.*) Yes. We started in the '30s and we just kept
on going. After we got the export market going and a greater share of
the Canadian production, we started to modernize the plant. God knows,
it needed it. We did jobs through the various mills, bringing them
up to a better state—the Rail Mill, the Blooming Mill, the Billet
Mill, Bar Mill, Rod Mill. Once we started getting a little money in
from our sales, we were at that—as fast as we built up profit from
sales, we spent it on the plant, to improve the efficiency.

We put in equipment to crush Wabana ore, which was the only
iron ore available to us in those days. I told you that it's a very
difficult ore to smelt in that it was so dense.

As we crushed this ore, we screened it, into three different
sizes. And each size would all charge separately into the Blast Furnace so that everything in each layer got smelted at about the same
rate. And *still* the "fines" could present some difficulty in that they're
liable to plug up the air trying to get up through. So we built a
sinter plant—fine ore was made into lump ore. And all this materi-
ally improved our Blast Furnace practice.

When I first came here they were using on the order of 2400
pounds of coke to make a ton of iron. By breaking the ore down
and separating it, we decreased the amount of heat required to do
the job. So we dropped the coke consumption down to in the order
of 1600 pounds per ton. That's efficiency.

(*And this is the result of capital investment to improve the plant
and modernize it.*) Well, I don't like the term "modernize." It improved the efficiency. To hell with this "modernization." You should
never have to modernize your plant, if you looked after it—be-

cause that's what you're doing all the time, keeping it modern.

(*So you're giving me a picture of a steel plant operated in such a way that when money was available, when profit was made, a percentage of that profit was plowed back into the plant to increase its efficiency.*) Well, we never paid any dividends, let's put it that way. All the money we made went back into the plants. And it wasn't until 1947 that we paid the first dividend from DOSCO— 25 cents a share. All the rest of the money went back in the plant. And in 1951 or '52, the dividend was increased to 50 cents—and that's where it stayed right up to the end.

(*By "the end" I take it you mean the purchase of DOSCO by A.V. Roe, later called Hawker-Siddeley. How did that come about?*) L. A. Forsythe was president. He became ill and died just before Christmas 1956. So here we were without a president. And the directors persuaded C. B. Lang to go back in as president, temporarily; he'd been president for just two years, before L. A. Forsythe.

A 90-ton ingot being loaded in the Open Hearth for shipment by rail to Trenton, Nova Scotia—to be used in the manufacture of rail cars.

He did—but from then on it was a question of what was to become of DOSCO. Do we find a new president, or what? Quite a few angles were looked at. And I am sorry to say that the one that was finally accepted was the offer of A.V. Roe to buy it out.

I was against it. It was against my desires and a lot more of us too, that had to do with the operations.

A.V. Roe didn't know anything about steelmaking. I don't know that I had this idea at the time, but it certainly came to me afterwards. They wanted to build up their Canadian holdings, make money on them, and then ship the money back to England. A.V. Roe—they later became Hawker-Siddeley—they were in bad shape in England. I was told by a man who was well-informed that they owed some 96 million pounds to the government and all they wanted to do was make money here in Canada and ship it to England for the benefit of A.V. Roe, Hawker-Siddeley, or whatever you like to call them. They had no real interest, other than that, in building Canadian industry at all.

Our main problem was to build this plant up so that it could operate efficiently—because God knows it had not been that way. I'm not talking about labour. Using those materials that I spoke about—the iron ore and coal we had—that did not permit of any great efficiency. Matter of fact, they had 5000-odd men working at that plant at one time. (*It got boiled down to 3000?*) Nearer 4000, I suspect. You had to. Going the way they were, they'd have ended in receivership again. (*So you do not agree that you could have diversified here and made the finished products here efficiently.*) No, I won't go that far. What do you mean? That the Wire and Nail Mill should still be there? (*Well, actually, that was one of the things the Union listed.*) I don't know how many times during my regime I'd be asked by somebody on the board of directors, well, why are you still making nails at that plant? And I produced figures once every few years or so to show that it was a good business.

You see, not all the steel you make will fit the purpose for which you made it. You get off-heats in the Open Hearth furnaces. A lot of that steel went into wire and nails, which are not particularly high-quality products—nails, anyhow. So you can divert something that you might have to remelt. So I was always able to argue against closing down the Wire and Nail Mill. (*But it* was *closed eventually.*) After my time.

(*While you were there—the efficiency of the plant keeps growing. In 1963, you get a production record of 796,000 tons. Then in '64, you're still there: 797,000 tons is hit. And the Blooming Mill breaks its own record. And the first Blast Furnace breaks the 12-month record. And they're doing it with a work force, not of 5000 but of 3000—gone down 2000 men in 20 years.*) Something like that, yes. (*So the plant seems like a good plant in the '60s.*) It was. (*Then what went wrong? Why does Hawker-Siddeley want out in 1967? What happened?*) Well, tell me why did they buy out a car company in Montreal and spend 18 million dollars and never open it again? They were incompetent. Absolutely incompetent people.

(*That's terrible. I mean, at least we want a reason, we want to be able to say that somebody made a mistake or they pulled out because they could squeeze more money out of the plant that way....*) They had not made a success of anything they had laid their hands on in Canada—Hawker-Siddeley. (*Could it have been to their benefit to lose?*) No. But they were incompetent people. (*You don't see it as malicious, as a back-room deal where a lot of money was made but the people of Sydney were hurt?*) No. Where would they make their money on that? By the government buying the plant, perhaps? They didn't make a hell of a lot there. I know that, because I was working with the government on it. Hawker-Siddeley sent their top legal man from Toronto down here during those proceedings, telling me that if I continued to buck them on the deal they wanted with the government, they would stop my pension.

(*You were an advisor to the government on the takeover?*) Yes. (*And at first Hawker-Siddeley wanted more than you thought they should receive?*) I think they asked the government originally for something like 25 million dollars. At the meetings that followed, I'd ask them awkward questions: "What are you going to do with the Rail Mill? It's shut down now. Why should anybody give you any money for that?" The raw materials they had, they had those all priced—I said, "They're not worth that, just sitting on the ground, and that's where they'll stay." So finally we got them down and paid them something like three million dollars. Between three and

four. And Hawker-Siddeley blamed me for most of that.

The tragedy was when Hawker-Siddeley came in the picture originally. They were completely incompetent. (*And your opinion has never changed on this?*) No. Reinforced it, if anything.

(*I wish you could say to me, "They saw a way to make money by letting the plant go down, and this was a smart boardroom business deal...."*) I don't know why they ever came to such a decision, craziest thing I ever heard of, group of so-called industrial people talking, making such silly decisions. (*To get out in 1967?*) Yes. To abandon this plant. (*And if they had held onto it, if they had treated it right, would we have the problems we're facing today?*) Not if they had been competent operators. In fact, on the contrary, if they had gone ahead as we decided originally, this plant would be making over a million tons every year. And it *did* make a million tons the first full year the government had it.

(*You put a tremendous amount in that plant.*) I gave my life to it, in effect. My working life. In 1945 they made me general manager of the whole thing, not coal. (*And you've stayed here.*) People used to ask me when I was getting around 60, "Where are you going when you retire?" Everybody else pretty well who had anything to do with the running of it, when they retired, they left here. I said, I'm going to stay right here. I don't know any better place in the world.

But as for the Steel Plant, I cut myself clear. Well, they put me on the board of directors for SYSCO, but I wasn't too happy there. (*Were you the only one on the board who knew how to make steel?*) Except for the president, and he didn't know too much about it. He had not gone through a life of steelmaking as I have.

CHAPTER 10

Black Friday and the Parade of Concern

On Friday, October 13, 1967—the day we call "Black Friday"—Hawker-Siddeley and DOSCO announced the closure of the Sydney Steel Plant. Fr. William Roach was at that time a Field Worker with the St. Francis Xavier University Extension Department. We talked to him in January 1990, on the day the Nova Scotia government wrote off the Steel Plant's debt. After years of government ownership, this seemed another step toward the sale of the Steel Plant to a private operator. The sale, however, never occurred.

But in 1967, Fr. Roach had served on the Citizens' Steering Committee that led to the November 19th Parade of Concern—the culmination of pressure that forced the Nova Scotia government to take over the Steel Plant that Hawker-Siddeley had abandoned. This helped to keep the Steel Plant alive until steelmaking in Sydney ended, in 2001.

We asked Fr. Roach, "Did you *know* that Black Friday was coming? Was closure of the Steel Plant in the air?"

FR. WILLIAM ROACH: No, no. Not at all. Not at all. Perhaps it should have been. But it wasn't. And there's a few reasons for it.

Coal was so much on our minds, that steel was not a concern. See, the "Donald Report" came out [a Royal Commission called *The Cape Breton Coal Problem*, headed by Dr. J. Richardson Donald]. I think it was in 1966. Black Friday was '67. And Donald recommended the closing out completely of the coal industry. And the coal industry was a much bigger employer: Glace Bay, New Waterford, and the Northside. And I think it was to close out about 1971, the last coal mine. But Donald was very strong in recommending measures to offset the social impact. He was very good on that respect.

And there was no question about it, it was as a result of Dr. Donald's suggestions on the social impact—and then, our pressure—that brought about DEVCO [Cape Breton Development Corporation]. Now, if DEVCO didn't work, a lot of it would be more our fault than anybody else's. The concept was good. And it certainly did a lot of good since it came on the scene—DEVCO. Everything wasn't perfect, but I don't know what we would have done without it.

And then, because of DEVCO, and because of people like Bill Marsh and others putting pressure on Allan MacEachen, who was sort of the godfather around here—that's when Lingan was opened, some years later. And the whole coal industry turned around completely.

But in 1966, you know, the coal industry was finished. It was gone. And there was no thought of a [mine at] Lingan....

So it was in that setting. And nobody was concerned about the Steel Plant. Because if you would check—Stanfield had just completed a provincial election some months before. And in his campaigning he was talking about the Steel Plant and its future. And I guess he was honest and sincere. Stanfield always had the reputation of being an honest, upright man. [Then] shortly after that election, he became the national leader of the Progressive Conservatives. And shortly after G. I. Smith took over [as Premier of Nova Scotia], we had Black Friday.

So, we had the politicians on our side. Because they claimed they had no idea it was going to happen. They had been told exactly the opposite [by Steel Plant management]. So they were angry. We were able to get some key leading politicians who were angry at the company. And that worked to our favour.

We had no idea that the Steel Plant was going to be closed. (*How did you first learn about it?*) It was a newscast, and I think it came from Montreal. And it came as a very clear, blunt statement— "It's going to close"—and the dates were all there. By the end of the year—1967, the current year— most of it would be closed down. And then there was a phase-out that would be complete by about April of '68—something like that. It was

Fr. William Roach

very clearcut. And there was no discussion about it, and there were no negotiations or anything. It was just a clear, blunt statement of closure.

The company was just apparently going to walk right out of it.

(*So you hear about the closure over the radio. What happens next?*) I think a couple of things happened. First, it was obvious from the [news] report that it was urgent. We had no time. The main closure was to take place at the end of December. So that's a little bit better than two months away. And I think it became quite clear to a number of people, that if the plant ever did close, you couldn't leave it closed for six months or a year and then try and get someone else to come in. The only way to keep it was to continue it. So there was an urgency.

And very clearly, with a group of us in the community—not many, there was only a small group of us—it became clear that it wasn't a steelworkers' problem. It was a community problem. And then we got the message loud and clear from some key people that this had to become a provincial problem. And then, it wasn't enough to make it a provincial problem. We had to make it a national problem. Because the solutions would have to be national and provin-

173

cial. Local you could take for granted—but local support was not enough to save the steel industry. So we worked....

(*Who is "we"? You said there was a small group of people.*) Yeah, it's a funny thing—funny thing, but since you called this morning, I was thinking about that. You know—a lot of them are not with us. Allan Sullivan became very active with us. I wouldn't doubt but that may have been Allan's reason for getting into politics later. He was a lawyer in Sydney. Ann Terry [MacLellan] was very active. And she was very helpful to us in the public relations and with the news media.

Vince Morrison—a Supreme Court judge, died about two years ago. Vince had been very active as a labour lawyer, and at one time had run on the CCF. It might have been NDP. Then later he ran on the Liberal ticket. But he was never elected. He didn't do much with us, but he did a few things; and he was a pretty sharp guy, good thinker. Sometimes it was great to have him at a meeting—he could get you zeroed in on the topic right quick.

Vince chaired the Parade of Concern meeting. It was big, and it was an outside meeting. And a powerful voice. He was sort of neutral, in a sense. He wasn't with the governments, he wasn't with the unions—he was neutral. A good chairman.

Dr. Neil Donovan—Neil's a psychiatrist—I think Neil is still around. He was in. And Sandy Campbell was involved with it. Sandy was *The Highlander* [a weekly newspaper in Cape Breton] at the time.

And then, quite a few other people. And all of our Extension crowd. Bishop Joe N. MacNeil was then the director of the Extension Department in Antigonish—he was my boss. And Fr. Topshee was the boss in the [Extension] office [in Sydney]. And I worked full-time on this, soon as Black Friday came. I wouldn't say on Friday, but by Monday I was full-time on it.

Then, there's a couple of people you may have run into—certainly you would know about them. Kingsley Brown, Sr. He was a journalist. And a fantastic storyteller, especially war stories. He was a prisoner-of-war during World War Two. But he, at the time, was working for St. F. X. in their development program. Doing some writing and public relations work. And Kingsley, Jr., was a

Part of the Citizens' Steering Committee. Left to right: Fr. William Roach; Mrs. Donovan; Bill Jessome, CJCB-TV; Mrs. Moraff; Martin Merner, president Local 1064 U.S.W.A., and chair of the Steering Committee; Mrs. Paruch, secretary; James Nicholson, director of District 2, U.S.W.A.; Vincent Morrison, Sydney barrister who chaired the Parade meeting; back to camera, Dr. Donovan. Missing members: Jeremy Akerman of CHER Radio; Mr. and Mrs. Doane Curtis, Jr.; Gus Dezagiacomo; and Evelyn Murphy.

CBC correspondent. And he had just recently left the CBC.

And through Fr. Topshee and myself, we were able to get both of them to move into Sydney for the month, practically, and work full time with the program to develop the March of Concern.

The idea, right off the bat—was to take it away from the Steelworkers Union, from a positive point of view. Because we *had* them. What we needed was broad community support. And then to get as much national publicity as possible. And that had to be through the news media—radio, television, newspapers.

And that's why we worked very closely with the *national* union leaders. Eamon Park came out of the national office [of the] Steelworkers Union. Bill Mahoney was the president. And he was very, very supportive of what we did. The research director—he was an economist—he came in and helped us a lot [Harry Weisblatt, the research director for the United Steelworkers of America].

And so the Steelworkers Union, locally, were in touch with us all the time. People like Eddie Johnston, Ben O'Neil. And Martin Merner was the president at the time.

Now, very early in the game it was clear that the federal government couldn't do anything directly, [such] as they were doing with the coal industry. You know, there was the big STELCO [steel] industry in Hamilton. There was no way that the federal government could take over a steel industry in Cape Breton. Whereas the coal, it was different.

The federal government could not politically take over the steel industry. So therefore it had to be the provincial. But the provincial couldn't do it financially. So you had to try and make a combination: the provincial do it, with as much [federal] financial backing—behind the scenes, indirectly—as possible. And that's what did take place.

(*I guess at the same time they were—or were they?—looking for a private owner for the Steel Plant.*) No, not then. There was no time. Two months, really. You're talking two months. The thing was to keep the plant going.

(*Was there a precedent? A steel plant in all of Canada that was run by a federal or a provincial government?*) No. No. No.

You know, you'd have to give Allan MacEachen strength, when he would go looking for support in Ottawa. And I think we did that.

And then, provincially, we had to sell it to G. I. Smith, and to the provincial people from Yarmouth and Halifax and Dartmouth.

(*Before you settled on a March of Concern, did you toy with any other options or any other ways of demonstrating?*) No, no, no. The March of Concern, I would say, developed out of everything we were doing. Contacting people, and interviews, TV, radio, newspapers. And as much publicity as possible. And: What would happen to the community if this plant closed? See, we were pushing hard on the consequences of the closure.

(*Any resistance in the Cape Breton community to this?*) None whatever. None whatever. There are people said, "You can't do it"—time of the year, you know. We were afraid, too. Because coming into November, in late November, in Cape Breton, you can run into some very bad weather. But we gambled—we had no choice.

We contacted everybody we could contact, through organizations. Whether they were unions, service clubs, political organizations, church groups. And we tried to get to the leaders. And from their leaders, to bring it down into—all political parties, all unions. Service clubs, everything. We would ask, let's say the Rotary Club and the Kiwanis Club of Sydney, "Let's see what you would do." And each group would take over some of the responsibility of making sure they got as many people to participate as possible. The UMW [United Mine Workers]—all of the unions.

Church groups were very active in it, all over the island. And we made sure that the bishops—the Anglican bishop had to come in, and our [Catholic] bishop had to come in. The head of the United Church for the Maritime Conference. So we had all of the leaders on our side, right early in the game. And that, of course, was funnelled down through the churches. The same with the unions, right down through the locals.

We hit hard on the politicians. I think almost every MP from Nova Scotia was in the Parade. And it would be Bob Muir that had the responsibility of making sure you dragged those guys in. Bob was the MP for this area, the Sydneys, at the time.

(*Did G. I. Smith really want the province to take over that*

Steel Plant?) I think he was scared to death of it. And we pressured him—no question about it. He had a great respect for Tom McKeough. I think Tom McKeough was the leading cabinet minister in G .I. Smith's government at the time. He would be the one, I think, that G. I. Smith would trust more than anybody else. Tom was a good man. You know, he was a good, kind—he had a feel for people. Might not have been the sharpest politician in Halifax. But he was a good man.

And then, "Pinky" Gaum was down at the Pier. And Pinky was in Cabinet. Gerry Doucet was in Cabinet. He was in Port Hawkesbury area. And he was a young, up-and-coming politician. And G.I. formed them into a committee. They were the committee to look after this particular crisis.

So Tom McKeough was the chairman. And I would think that G.I. was scared of it. But we pressured G. I. Smith. He would not have been able to back off easily.

(*What could you say to G. I. Smith, to convince him?*) The social impact. You know—what's going to happen to Sydney? At that time—you know, there was no great College of Cape Breton, either. And there was no Coast Guard College. A lot of things that we now have, we didn't have then. It was more a one-horse town then than it is now. We didn't have the services developed as well then as we do now.

You know, [now] you have Point Edward, and you have the Industrial Park, and you have the Coast Guard College, you have a developed college out the highway out there—the University College of Cape Breton. You have more nursing homes—the hospitals are bigger and better, and the new one coming [Cape Breton Regional Hospital]. You have many more developed services now in Cape Breton County than you did in 1967. Well, I suppose that is common to any part of Canada. But that was the fact.

(*But had the Steel Plant failed then, the prospects of any of this other coming....*) Would have been very slim. Oh, well, on a reduced basis—much reduced basis. Including the College. (*Including the population.*) Sure. Oh, absolutely. There was a heavy out-migration in the 1950s and '60s, in Cape Breton County.

See, when I went to school—my last days going to school in

The Parade enters the Sport Centre—the present-day racetrack at Tartan Downs

New Waterford, there were three mines operating. And I suppose there must have been 2400 to 3500 men working in the coal mines. That had all disappeared [by 1967]. I can remember—I used to be embarrassed—and I'd get angry with some of the government people we often worked with in Extension, working in New Waterford. And the main street is Plummer Avenue. And they used to refer to it as "Plywood Avenue," because it was all boarded up. Because people were moving.

So you could see a similar pattern happening in Sydney. With coal and steel gone—both of them—well, what was left in industrial Cape Breton? Nothing but the service industries that were supporting the coal and steel, or were supported by the coal and steel.

(*And this was the kind of pressure you would bring to G. I. Smith.*) Right. (*And hoping that he and his government would care enough about Cape Breton to take a leap that no government had ever taken before.*) Yes.

(*And he was pressured from the federal level, or was he just*

179

Views from the Steel Plant

told, "If you make this decision, you'll be funded"?) I think the federal government was scared to death.... But Allan MacEachen— you know, whatever you say about him, he did have a strong social conscience, and he did feel he had a responsibility for Cape Breton. And he and Tom McKeough, I'm positive—behind the scenes— worked very closely together.

Now, they wouldn't come out. But I know that right after the takeover, the federal government bought the Coke Ovens. Well, the federal government needed a coke ovens like I needed a hole in the head. But it was a way of giving several million dollars to the provincial government immediately, to help them with the takeover. I forget what the amount was, but it was five or six million dollars. And that money was immediately given to the provincial government to use in their takeover, running the plant.

And there were other things the federal government did. The federal government had just made loans to the steel company for the building of a new wharf system down in the Pier. And that was owed to the federal government. And that was written off immediately.

So there were a number of things like that, that the federal government were able to do—indirectly—that helped pay for the takeover.

(*Was the Parade of Concern the only—what would we call it?— kind of act that was taken? Was it the only performance?*) No. It was constant on TV and radio for two months. We tried to get as much.... Programs—I don't know what the programs were then because, remember, this is 1967. And television certainly wasn't as developed as it is in 1990. But programs similar to "The Journal"—that type of program—we made sure we got someone on that....

And on the CTV—whatever the leading programs were at the time. And that type of thing. (*And radio, here?*) Oh, radio right across the country—right across the country.

And it was easy to hit the company—it was a foreign company—to be fair. You know, it was foreign ownership, and look what they did to us. And that lent itself for community support.

180

And they had no consideration for us whatever. And their announcement was so blunt that it helped our cause.
(*Were you looking for any long-range promise from the government?*) No, no. (*If they chose to operate it for a few months and
find a new buyer, a private buyer—you didn't care.*) We were not
even considering that. (*So it wasn't a question of, "We don't want it
to be an independent entrepreneur running it."*) No. (*You didn't
care, as long as it stayed operating.*) Right. (*And, based on that
then, you would look for other solutions.*) Right.

(*The reason I say that is because some people complain that
the government was never really committed to public ownership.*)
That might be true. There was an immediate problem that required
an immediate solution, and there was no time to go look for a private operator.

But in the meantime, something had to be done.

(*Okay. Tell me about the Parade of Concern.*)
The Parade of Concern was well, well organized. We never
had a parade like that in eastern Nova Scotia, before or since. And
the time of the year. And we changed in time where we were going
to hold it. We thought we'd have a big meeting in the Sydney Forum. And we were not long into the preparation when we realized
Sydney Forum could not hold what we were planning for. We had
no facility. And the only thing we could think of was the Sport
Centre [the present-day racetrack at Tartan Downs]. And that's totally open-air. You know, even the stands at the Sports Centre were
open-air—they're closed in now. But they were wide open. And
that's the only thing we had. We didn't have any other choice.

And then how to get people to the Sports Centre was another
problem. So all of that had to be worked out. And where we would
start. And crowd control. We ran into all of these problems that we
had no idea were part of organizing a major parade. And we had a
lot of help from police and RCMP, news media. The unions were
tremendous, all of the unions. The schools. We had all the schools
involved.

And parking and buses—many of the people parked at Woolco,
for example, and places like that. People from away, they never

came into the city at all, with cars. There was no way that they could all come in. So we had trains and buses and everything all lined up to move the crowd into the starting point, which was over by the Steel Plant, to march up Prince Street....

And we ran into a whole lot of things that we didn't anticipate. We never realized how long it would take to bring 20 or 30—whatever number it was—thousands of people into the Sports Centre through one main gate. So it took more than an hour, or an hour and a half—two hours, I suppose—from the time the first ones landed at the Sports Centre until the end of the Parade finally got into the Sports Centre.

And it had rained heavy all Saturday night, and stopped about 10:30, 11 o'clock Sunday morning—heavy rain. So they were standing in mud, literally. You know, you were walking in mud. And after a while it didn't matter if you didn't have rubbers on, or you were going over your shoes. It was just a big field out in the centre of the Sports Centre, inside the track. That's where everybody was standing.

But it worked well. And there was a good feeling. I think everybody was happy that there was such a large turnout. The spirit was good, and there was no anger. And it was all organized—the speeches—that they would be quick, to the point—get started, get over, and get out. And a little bit of entertainment in between. Waiting for the crowds to fill up.

Vince Morrison chaired the meeting, and everything was quick, to the point, then it was finished, then we all left. So there was no anger. Because there was no [steel] company [present]. It was all ourselves, and we were trying to impress government. And we impressed them. We had news media from all over the country. It was a tremendous turnout.

(*And where were you that day?*) I was in the beginning of the Parade, early, because I was involved—and I had to speak. There were only five speakers. And only one from the community—only one local speaker. That was me. And that was agreed upon by the committee. And it was only short—maybe a five-minute speech. The two big speeches were G. I. Smith and Allan MacEachen. Not in length, but that's where the power was. We had someone from

the CLC [Canadian Labour Congress] in to speak. And someone from the United Steelworkers in from the head office. Nobody local. It was the outside support that we needed. And the real pressure was to be on G. I. Smith and Allan MacEachen. Allan speaking for the federal government, and G.I., of course, the Premier. It was geared to that.

(*Did G.I. have the answer that day?*) No. He didn't have the answer. And there was no question about it, they were playing one against the other, in a sense—feeling one another out—Allan and G. I. Smith. They both knew they had to do something, because they were not going to get off the hook. And I'm sure they didn't know exactly. But it developed quickly.

And I know the decision was made very soon after that. Because the government was supposed to take over on the first of January. They actually took over, in practice, about the fifth or tenth of December. Because all of the [steel company] management, locally, were on our side. We had a unique situation, that the management people and union people were together. And they were doing in December what they knew they should be doing for the takeover at the first of January.

Views from the Steel Plant

(*Hawker-Siddeley did finally sell the plant to the provincial government. Is that correct?*) Very little selling. It was almost a takeover. They were closing it out anyway, and abandoning the plant. It wasn't as if they were going to transfer very much of it to anywhere. So, they were leaving it for nothing. So why could they now sell it, when they didn't even *try* to sell it! I think that the government had that.... And I don't think that there was much money involved....

So there was quite an effort of working together to try and find the solution. Without anybody knowing what the solution was. I'm sure they had no idea what they were going to get into. Maybe it was better that they didn't!...

(*So the province took over a plant that needed modernization.*) Yes. Absolutely. Yes. (*But it did not modernize.*) It did not modernize. (*And sometimes it partially modernized.*) Yes. (*But....*) Never really. (*There was never—if I can say it like this—you correct me every time I'm wrong, please. It seems there was never a commitment to operate that plant at its best.*) No. (*Am I correct?*) That's right. (*By making the investment that would bring it up to state-of-the-art.*) That's right. And both governments—Liberal and Progressive Conservative both. (*You know, they put in a portion of this and that—but there was never the commitment....*) To modernize the steelmaking facility.

When they took it over first, they had to do it. It was an immediate thing. There was no time to play around with "maybe we will or maybe we will not." If the plant had closed, and it was left closed for six months or a year, it would never have re-opened. That's my opinion.

So it was an immediate thing. We're talking two months. Let's take it over now. And after we take it over, and it's continuing, then maybe we'll find a way out. But they were not looking for that way out. That was not part of the original takeover. Just do it. And we'll answer that question.... And they never answered the question. Year after year after year after year.... (*Right. They neither sold it, nor modernized it.*) That's right. For 22 years, 23 years.

(*And I guess we don't want to take away from the fact that we still have Sydney.*) That's right, and we wouldn't have had it. (*And*

184

Charlie MacKinnon
at the Parade of Concern

Let's Save Our Industry

CHORUS: Let's Save Our Industry
Let's Save Our Industry
Let's Save Our Industry—
The industry we need.

It brought us joy and brought us tears.
It's been here over sixty years.
It built our homes and stilled our fears
And made this island what it is. CHORUS

We need the help of Ottawa,
We are also part of Canada.
They can subsidize Ontario,
Expo and the Seaway too. CHORUS

We stand united one and all,
The Maritimes must never fall.
So let's all get behind the wheel
And save our coal and save our steel. CHORUS

Sherry MacKinnon MacNeil, *Charlie's daughter*: "He was so wrapped in the moment, and so enthused, that when he tried to stop, his hands and his knuckles and his fingers were almost freezing from the cold. It was so cold. And it was an effort to play that guitar. But the people just wanted more and more. And they were carrying on the song, and consequently, he had to keep going. And then he got wrapped up in it, and he said, half the time he wasn't even thinking of it—when he'd go to slow down, he'd feel his fingers again. They'd freeze, trying to strum the guitar. It was so intense."

(*When did your dad actually make that song?*) "'Let's Save our Industry?'—the night before the Parade of Concern. He got a call from Martin Merner, president of the Steelworkers Union at that time. And he asked Dad if he could think of something to get the people going, to keep them there—everybody enthused, and everybody could be together. And he came up with it the night before. And my mother was with him when he wrote it at the kitchen table."

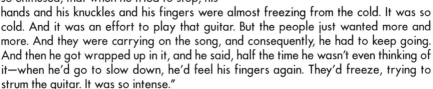

a much more developed Sydney.) Much more. (*Than you were faced with in 1967.*) Right....

Some funny things happened [at the Parade of Concern]. We never had a crowd like that before, so we had no experience. We were hoping that there would be no trouble. And people had told us there might be trouble. Because there was anger. You know, your whole community's gone. And we intentionally—this is no accident—we put that starting point—and we argued about that, and we made sure—over at the beginning of the Steel Plant. Rather than Victoria Park. So we wouldn't have to come through the business district. And we went right down Inglis Street, out. And there was really no place or reason for any violence in that parade. And it was long enough to keep people busy. You had to walk a couple of miles, see. That was all intentional—that wasn't accidental. That was for crowd control and anger control.

And then when we got to the Sports Centre, it was so long to try and get them in. Because there was no parking—it was just the inside of a big field. (*This is the racetrack.*) It was just in the centre, in the field. Just a level type of an old swamp, that's all it was. And we were up on this stand. And never really had prepared for an hour-and-a-half to two-hour wait. The Men of the Deeps were there to sing a few things.

But MacKinnon was there—Charlie MacKinnon. And he was a steelworker, and he played the guitar and he used to sing these western, country-type music songs. He made up a little song. (*And was that prepared?*) No! He had it written—the words written on the back of an Export A cigarette package: "Let's Save Our Industry." And he started that. And my God, the people joined in. And that really took off. There was no preparation for that. And the darn thing took off. We had nothing else to do, anyway. And the crowd all got in on the chorus. And it really worked.

You know, it was just a pure accident.

And they were playing that all over Canada on TV and radio. Now, after that it was perfected a little, and Charlie would have gone through it again with a better setting. But right in the crowd, with—whether it was 15- or 20-thousand people—waiting for the last thousand to come in—in mud. They were all singing. Everybody was singing. And Charlie was standing up there.

And Vince Morrison was sharp—he sensed right quick that this was catching on. So he let Charlie front stage, up in front of the mike, play it as long as he could play it, to hold the crowd together. Then the speeches came very quick, and not long. And they were over, and that's it—everybody went home.

Oh, Charlie stole the show! Because the crowd got in on it. It was cold and wet and damp. So they all started to sing. And that was not planned—that was just pure accident.

(*And when you say they went home—they just wandered out of the place? That was just the end of it?*) Yeah, m-hm. (*They felt they had done their job.*) Yeah. (*No promises, though.*) No promises, no.

That's why I say, the meeting afterwards—the meeting, I remember, with Marchand and Pépin and Allan MacEachen— I'm sure that was after. Because the meetings were fast and furious. And I know that Tom McKeough—and they had agreed—the management agreed—[the province] took over the Steel Plant, practically, in December.... And legally, they took it over the first of January. And they didn't pay any attention to the far-away management, whoever they were. It was an immediate takeover—not legally, but practically.

(*That's interesting. The whole thing is interesting. It's interesting how the government was pulled into it, and that's really all we were fighting for at that point—get them into it, and see what we do with it down the road.*) That's right. Not even looking down the road. We can't handle that now, we've got too much of a problem right here. Let's do it.

(*How long was the Parade of Concern, by the way?*) I would say we started at 12:30. Sunday afternoon. And it was all over at 4:30—4, 4:30. Most of the time was spent in getting up there. And once we got them all in, I would say it only lasted an hour.

(*Anything else happen that was funny or unusual or...?*) No. The Charlie MacKinnon one was funny, though. I was up there with him, you know—there were a few of us up there. And, "Drive 'er, Charlie!" you know. And Charlie just rose to the occasion. You couldn't believe the spirit out there. We could see everybody, of course—we were up in the stand. And there was a very friendly spirit. And that was great for us, because we were somewhat worried that they might get out of control, you know. There wasn't even a chance of it, the way it developed.

(*Where has that spirit gone, Fr. Roach? How come we're not screaming today?*) I'm not too sure. Now, I don't know. But maybe, when the government has it—where there's a problem, "Well, okay, do something." See, in those days, the government didn't have coal. And the government didn't have steel. So there was no automatic answer. And we had to fight for an answer. We had to look for an answer. But since the takeover—"Well, it's your steel plant—you look after it. If it's a problem, you look after it." And the coal industry, the same thing. But up until that time, remember, it wasn't government. The government didn't have the coal mines. And they didn't have the Steel Plant. So it was a different type of a—maybe.

(*And today...?*) "You have to do it. You're government."

CHAPTER 11
Winston Ruck, Steelworker

December 27, 1940, I consider as the happiest day of my life.

December 27 is when I got a job at the Steel Plant. I will never forget that day as long as I live. Because at that time we had been living with my aunt, from the time my father had passed on in 1936. And that was the height of the Depression. Very difficult. Not only for ourselves, but for everybody. Including the white community as well. Those were difficult times.

As I indicated, we five boys—five brothers—were living with my aunt [Mrs. Viola Calender] following the death of my father. Her husband was working on a part-time basis.

You can imagine the load that they suddenly found themselves with, with the advent of five boys—hungry boys with appetites! But we were—like I said, we were resourceful because we were taught that way, from the time we were small, to look after yourself. And we used to help the best we could, by going up to the old Marsh Dump and bringing home coal during the summer months, to help. Because it was hard for them to find the money to buy a ton of coal. A half ton cost $2.50 in those days. That was hard to come up with, that $2.50. Now, we weren't the only ones that did it. All the other boys in the community did the same thing. That was their way of assisting their families. Go up to the Marsh Dump.

You'd pick the coal from the dump. We carried them on our backs. We weren't very big or we weren't very strong. But we managed to bring coal down to keep the house going all winter without them having to purchase coal.

And the same with the wood supply, we looked after that. And they had a few chickens and a few ducks there. That was our job, to feed them. They would kill them off, particularly around Christmas time or Easter time. And things of that nature.

And that was our way of making a contribution to the house. And Mr. Calender, my aunt's husband, he appreciated that very, very much. He used to always tell us. As a matter of fact, he even built an additional shed so we could put more coal in.

And so, I was getting older. I used to get an odd job here and there. I used to go around assisting people in building homes, basements. Take the wheelbarrow and help pour the concrete. The city was putting through a sewer and a waterline on Maloney Street, back in the late '30s. And I got a job on that. On digging. Pick and shovel. Hard, hard work. I was only about 15, 16 at the time.

And that was a tough digging, because there was a lot of rock going up the hill. All rock. They had to dynamite continually to break through the rock.

So those were the things that we did at that time. I was going to the Academy, in Grade 10, Grade 11. Then during the summer months, that's what we would do.

I also worked on the beer truck. My father was a very prominent man and managed to secure the contract for hauling the beer to the Pier. Billy Hill—another prominent Liberal at that time—

had the contract for the town liquor store. There were only two at that time. So after my father died, his partner carried on with that. And occasionally I'd get a job in a truck, hauling beer. And then, when he had no hauling, I'd get a job with Billy Hill.

So while we were working hauling the beer, you'd go down to the General Office [at the Steel Plant]. Because the General Office started to hire people then in late '39 and '40, because of the war. And we put our name in during the summer—all of us did at that time.

And in order for you to get a job, you had to be there when they called your name. You used to sit around out there for a couple of hours. But you couldn't do that every day because some days you probably got another job and you've gone someplace else, or you've gone to play ball. And that would be the day they came out and they call off your name. If you weren't there, they forgot about you. They hired whose name they called up was there. That's the way that worked.

So this day in question, I had my name in for quite some time, all that summer. They were hiring people sporadically, here and there. December 27, 1940, I was working for Billy Hill. And a call came down to the dispatcher, the agent for CN—he checked all the beer that was taken off the cars. Man by the name of Bricky Williams. My aunt had called him and told him that they wanted me at the General Office. Get up to the General Office. I assumed that they were going to hire me.

I jumped off the car, grabbed my hat and coat jacket. And I ran all the way to the General Office because, like I said, if you

Winston's father, George Ruck, holding Arthur; children left to right: Vernal Braithwaite (step-brother), Winston, Calvin, Lionel

didn't get there that day, forget it. And I never had that much time. And I got there. Got into the door of the hiring officer. And I was the only one there—it was pretty near quitting time.

And I got in, I was huffing and puffing. I remember Cecil MacPherson saying to me, "Son, you're all in." I said, "Yes." I said, "I ran all the way in here." "Well," he said, "sit down, sit down." I was all in. He gave me a chair to sit down. And he went in and got my card and number. He said, "Don't worry," he said, "we're going to hire you."

I'm telling you, those were the greatest words I ever heard in my life.

(*Why?*) To get a job! (*Well, you had a job.*) Oh, yeah, but this job we had was only sporadic. You may get two days this week. That was the most you could get. (*And how good a job were you going to get at the Steel Plant?*) A steady job working seven days a week! You were going to get a steady job, in the Steel Plant. So you were sure of a pay every week. And you're getting the wages that they paid at that time, which was $3.63 a day, I think it was. It was 43$\frac{1}{2}$ cents an hour—do the arithmetic on that. (*It's $3.48 a day.*) Seven days a week. Seven days a week. You had to work seven days to get you a $20 bill. 'Cause they had to take off for benefits at that time, and some other deductions that they made.

So in order for you to see a $20 bill—my eyes were like that! Twenty dollars to me! In my pay bag! When I got my first seven days and saw $20 in a pay envelope that belonged to me! Merciful heaven, that was—talk about being on Cloud Nine.

But I got ahead in my story. So, he hired me that day. He said, "I'm not even going to bother to send you for an examination. It's too late. But you come back Monday morning and we'll send you in to see Dr. Lynch"—was the company doctor at that time. And they had a little clinic hospital right there, next to the General Office. But he gave me my clock card and, best of all, he gave me my check number—1057. That was my number. Look, I was so grateful. "I thank you, I thank you, I thank you. Very very much." Now I've got a check number in my hand.

And when he gave me that, and—opened the door for me. By this time everybody was pretty well gone now. It was getting on to

General Office, Steel Plant, demolished 1990

5 o'clock, and they generally closed around 4:30, so I was pretty close—I just got in under the wire.

I took that and I ran all the way home. I came bursting in the door, and I said, "Aunt Vee, Aunt Vee, I got hired! Here's my check number. I've got to go to work tonight, on the backshift." This was 11 to 7 then.

And she was so grateful. She hugged me, and she cried. And she went out—she said, "Okay," she put on her coat. She went up to the store—one of the merchants, Jewish merchants, in the Pier. Whatever money she made, she bought me overalls and boots, work gloves, and—socks, and a lunch can.

And I went to work that night on the backshift. I was 17 years old, 17$^1/_2$. Talk about gladness and happiness—that was it. And of course, everybody, all my other brothers and two cousins, were all happy because I got the job, because now I could visualize that I would be able to ease the finances of the household. Well, five boys!

(*What was this job that you had gotten?*) This job was in the Steel Plant—just a labourer. (*Which meant?*) Which meant that I was going to get a steady pay every week. (*But what did it mean that you were going to do? What does "just a labourer" do?*) Well, really, I didn't know until I went there. I had no idea. (*You still didn't know what your job....*) I had no idea. I was just being hired on the Steel Plant. That's all we knew—we were hired on as a steelworker. And so you go wherever they direct you. That's what it was. You go wherever—you were getting a job.... I didn't know nothing! I knew that there were these different departments, all right. That's just because you heard them being spoken about in the community.

So I went to work that night. Didn't know how to find my way in to where I had to go. (*You'd never been into the Steel Plant?*) No. No. (*Lived there all your life but you'd never been....*) No. I had no real idea—you couldn't get in. How were you going to get in? (*Oh, I see, your father worked there, but you couldn't go into the Steel Plant.*) No. I was down where he worked. I used to take sometimes his lunch down to him, where he worked in the Brick Plant. But that was just one little section. You go across the track, and you're right in there. (*So this was a new place to you.*) This was down in the main part of the plant. (*You'd never been in there.*) They weren't allowing any kids, any boys, to go in there. Only ones that got in there were people who were employed in the plant and going to work. So there was no way you could get in there beforehand. They had watchmen on the gates. So it was inaccessible to people.

So I knew that I had to go in through the gate right by where the overpass is there—used to be a subway then. And when I went in that gate, I asked the watchman where this place I had to go to—department called the General Yard Department. But I was fortunate enough that while I was going into work—there was a man who knew my father. And he was a foreman in the department where I was going. So fate always somehow manages to play his hand—has a role in these things. And he knew my father well. Freddy Robinson. And he said, "Well, come on with me, Ruck," he said. "I'm going there."

And he took me down, through all the shortcuts. There's no way I would ever have found that place by my own. 'Cause the watchman was giving me the long way, which would be the most simple way. But Robinson—he took me through the mills, here and there shortcuts—that's the most direct way. Up and down the ladder, in this building, open that door....

I went into a little office, there was a fellow sitting behind a chair.

His name was Dan Burke. I gave him my card and he took it. And he took my number down—1057. The big building where all the fellows that were coming to work—a lot of new people were hired that day. And I sat with that group. There were others who had been working for some time, were there. Then finally he came out.

And all of us fellows that were hired that day, he told us to go down to the Open Hearth Department. We didn't even know where the Open Hearth Department was. And it was dark—pitch dark. There was no great amount of streetlights on there, you had to feel your way and follow somebody who knew where they were going. This was at nighttime—11 o'clock.

Went in the Open Hearth Department. And talk about being frightened—seeing these big furnaces, and flames shooting out all over—and coming at you. And the noise of the overhead cranes, the charging cars, and people walking. You're scared to death! You had to walk between these furnaces in order to go where we were going. And the flames sometimes would be shooting out from the gas.

Anyway, we went in there—somebody guided us in. And the foreman came. He took the loan sheet that somebody had. He told us where to put down our lunches and hang up our coats. He knew we were all brand-new men—young boys. Eight of us or ten of us.

And he put us to work cleaning up the tracks—the slag off the tracks. Throwing it into an old pan. And cranes would come and lift it up and carry it away and dump it. And we were just terrified. Terrified, you know. You have to be careful. 'Cause things are moving on tracks. The train'd be coming in this door—backing in, you know. The foreman was very, very careful with us. He knew we were all [new]—he would watch us. First thing you know, there's a crane car, you know—a ladle of steel. And sparks were flying! And he'd say, "Go on inside there for a while." And we'd go in there, and then he'd go in and call us out.

That was quite an experience—shocking to me. Trains coming in to take out the steel. A side door—you might be standing there, all of a sudden you hear, "Bwooo! Bwooop!" You didn't know what direction it was coming from. But after a while you became familiar with where you had to go; where you should walk and where you shouldn't walk. He was very kind to us.

That was my first shift that night, and I put it in. Sleepy, and tired, of course, after working all day. But still happy and elated that I was working.

(*And coming out after your first day's work....*) That was my first time that I actually saw inside the Steel Plant. We had seen the Steel Plant from the outside, walking by it on the way. Going up to Ashby, you had to walk by the Wire and Nail Mill. But it was fenced in—you couldn't see over it. Some of the buildings would be above the fence.

And you could see the Coke Ovens, going up Victoria Road. And you could see other parts of the plant if you were down the tracks, on the way to town, or going by the General Office. On the way over to Victoria Park to watch a ball game. You saw a few buildings there, but that's all you saw, just from the outside.

(*And each day, you would go to General Yard.*) See, the various departments would call the General Yard for extra help. So, for example, if the Blooming Mill required some extra men for jobs within the Blooming Mill Department, they would call up. When you get over there, they will put you in the various jobs that are open at that time. It was basically labour work. (*Next day you might be in the Open Hearth?*) Or the Blast Furnace. Or the Coke Oven. Or the Bar Mill. You know.

You would work yourself into a job within the mill context, too, mind you. You weren't just only using a broom or a shovel or a pick. Sometimes you'd go up and they'd place you in a job as part of that department.

There were various, numerous jobs in connection with the operation of that department. So you were considered as extra help to fill in for people who perhaps reported off sick for one reason or another—filling these jobs to keep the operation going.

I was in the General Yard for about close to a year. Then I went over to the mill's boilers—they made the steam for the Blooming Mill. It's like a boilerhouse. So I worked there for—oh, up until the time I went into the Army, I suppose, in '43....

[In the Army] we had some of the same aspects that occurred during the First War happen in the Second World War. They were not too keen on accepting blacks in the service. I wasn't old enough to go into the service at the time it started in '39. In '39 I was 16. But there were several black men who applied, not only here in Sydney but throughout Nova Scotia and other parts of Canada, who were turned down. Turned down because of race.

So that went on for quite a while. I suppose as they got further down into the war, they decided to change that policy, because they needed every able-bodied man they could get. So that gradually disappeared as far as the service was concerned. And that policy held through. And the other parts of the service, like the Navy—I don't know of any blacks that were ever in the Navy. And there were very few in the Air Force. Very few.

(*Were any of your officers black?*) No. The only black officer I saw was a Capt. Oliver. Dr. William Oliver, out of Halifax. He was a clergyman. I don't know of any others that were black. I never saw them.

They never separated us or segregated us. You know, I went where everybody else did and did what everybody else did. I was expected to do it, you know. It wasn't something that I thought about while I was in the service....

(*Was the Steel Plant the same way, do you think?*) Yes. Much the same. They did it very, very covertly. But there were some areas where you knew that they didn't want you. For example, you knew you couldn't get a job in a machine shop, or the Electrical Department. The Railroad—Railroad was a very discriminatory department. They had that old system where they believed that they were the elite of the working class. That came from England. Practiced in the United States, too. They were the top of the line in the labour movement, the brotherhood. They even had various discriminatory tactics within that. For example, if you were in the Railroad and you were, let's say, a fireman. Well, you may go from fireman to driving. But you could never be a conductor. The only body who could be a conductor would be those who were on the footboard. They could go from there to conductor.

So that was discriminatory. We had to break that on the Steel Plant. That was part of the old brotherhood system.

(*Around the time of the Second World War—all these people who were on the Railroad in the Steel Plant....*) Were white. Every single one of them. We never even aspired to get that job because we knew we couldn't get it.

And they were discriminatory religious-wise. Indeed it was. As a matter of fact, in some parts of the plant, they were called— well, the R.C. were strong in the Open Hearth Department. Because the people who were in charge hired people who were R.C.'s. Do you understand how they could do it? And they exclude somebody who they know to be a Protestant. I'm not saying everybody down there was R.C. But it was dominant. And the same thing applied on the Railroad—the Protestants were dominant. R.C.'s never had a chance.

Once they found out your religion, they just discriminated against you automatically. What were you going to do about it? In order for you to get a job, you had to go to the superintendent. Superintendent already knows your background. Because in those days you had to put down what your religion was on your application! *Winston chuckles.*

[Today], that's against the law. Religion, or colour—they can't do that. I'm not saying they don't. But I mean, legally. It's not contained there [in the application]. But if you wanted to discriminate against me, and I made out this application—all you've got to do is put down the word "black." All you had to do is mark a certain notation, an "X" denotes black. Or circle. (*Like a little code.*) That's right.

I'm saying that they can do these things, and you wouldn't know. Because they're not telling me they're not hiring me because I'm black. They're saying they've got somebody else. They find a reason. There are some that would tell you, too, that, you know, "You can't get the job there because they don't hire blacks."

(*And the Machine Shop?*) Couldn't get there—that was basic Protestant. Protestant hire. And white—they had to be Anglo-Saxon. Highly discriminatory.

(*We're talking about people who have unions.*) That's right. (*They have brotherhoods.*) Yes. (*But those unions and brotherhoods permitted this.*) That's right. So it's not necessarily always the company. All the company was concerned with, who was going to do the work. The company, and I think primarily, were interested in getting production.

But there were company officials who were prejudiced—let's

Winston Ruck, Steelworker

December 18, 1968: A new yearly production record of 841,000 tons of steel ingot. In front of the control panel of Number 6 Open Hearth that day were (front row, left to right) Winston Ruck, Open Hearth manager Joe McIsaac, Joseph Zac, Stephen Humenick, and (back row) Harold Kirton, Chesley Porter, Peter Marenick, John Nalepa, Gar Campbell, and Mike Kowalchuk.

face it. The same as there were union officials who were prejudiced. There were company foremen that were prejudiced. There were company general foremen that were prejudiced. There were company superintendents that were prejudiced. So therefore if they're prejudiced, the people that they've got under them are going to be naturally the same way, because they know exactly why they were there. He's not going to hire somebody who is going to go against his wishes, is he? And put them in a position of authority. There's no way. 'Cause you would defeat his whole purpose. If he's determined that this is going to be all Catholic or all Protestant, he's going to make sure that people like the general foreman underneath him or the assistant superintendent, hire people that he wants there. If they have to belong to the Orange Lodge or the Masonic, or the Knights of Columbus. All those charitable orders

199

played a big role in the hiring practices of the Steel Plant. Depending on the official who was there....

(*So along comes Winston Ruck.*) It didn't matter where I was from. I could have been an R.C., or I could have been an Anglican or a United or a Presbyterian. That was not a consideration. If you were black.... (*That came first?*) That's right. Well, you're visible. My religion didn't mean a damn thing.

(*Excited as you were about getting on the Steel Plant, you knew that your opportunities were limited.*) Not necessarily. I was just interested in getting a job. A job. That was not a big consideration—"I want to go into the Steel Plant and I want to become a carpenter." I just wanted a job.

(*As you progressed in the Steel Plant—after you came back from the Second World War—you knew then that opportunities would be limited.*) Yes. I was aware then, because I was older. Understand. And I knew then for sure there were certain departments that we could not aspire to get a job in. I knew that, for example, one particular general foreman was a very, very prejudiced man. Everybody knew that. No if's, and's, or but's about him. And he was hard on black people—very hard. And if some black person got into some difficulty, he seemed to blame every black person for that. As if we were all responsible.

But he was prejudiced before I got on the plant, because I heard about him. And he was a very powerful man. You didn't stand up to him. His word was law.

The only body higher than him was the superintendent; but he was one that wielded the power—the day-to-day power. He would be the guy that would be responsible for day-to-day discipline. If it came to his attention that you left the job early, for example, he's going to deal with you the next time he sees you.

(*What do you mean by "deal with you"?*) Oh, he would shame you in front of a lot of people. He'd call you and he'd give you an awful going over. Boy, you got a tongue-lashing from him. You didn't want to go back for a second dose. No sir-ee. He dressed you down something terrible. And he would send you home. "You don't come back until I call you."

Or else if he wanted to discipline you, he'd tell you, "Now, you go home, and don't come out no more until the backshift. And you stay on the backshift." That was his way of disciplining. And you wouldn't get any work any place else. If he sentenced you to the backshift, you stayed on the backshift. You'd have a hard, hard time—'cause every time he saw you he would remember you. And he knew he put you on the backshift. I don't know how you could get out of it, 'cause you dare not go and ask him. You had to find another department who were looking for extra men, in order to beat the rap.

(*What's interesting to me is this: through all of this, you had a union at the Steel Plant.*) Yeah, union wasn't very strong in those days. Not prior to the end of the war, the union was not all that strong. And it depends on who your union representatives were. If you've got union representatives who are of good will, a lot of the things that the foremen would do, they wouldn't get away with it. If he had the gall and the guts to challenge them. There weren't too many like that at that time. Few and far between. So although we had the union, it wasn't all that strong.

But it became stronger and it became a force after the war. That's when I became interested in the union, in 1956.

(*What do you think changed you, what made you take an interest in the union?*) Because I had a good friend, named Frank Smith, who later became financial secretary during my presidency. We both were elected at the same time in 1970. And a funny thing about it is, how fate.... I'm getting off the other story kind of, 'cause there's lots more to be said about discrimination and I don't want to lose this thought while I have it in my mind.

Simply this—that Frank Smith was a well-respected man. I knew Frank—six or seven years older than I. But I remember him going to school. A fellow that we always had a great deal of respect for. He was a very ardent labour man. Did a lot of reading. Very intelligent. And he always was interested in the labour movement. He could remember the strike in 1923 for example. I was only born in '23. Frank, he remembered those Mounted Police chasing the people. That remained in his mind. And he wrote a book based on what he saw as a boy, to the steelworkers [*Brief History of Local 1064 United Steelworkers of America and Its Achievements*]. He used to urge me all the time to come and attend the meetings, and so on and so forth.

And finally in 1956 he came, along with others—"Winston, why don't you let your name stand for nomination, and run for the Grievance Committee, steward"—of the General Yard Department. So I did, along with another good friend of mine named Johnny MacDonald, who's since passed on as well. So that's how I became interested in the union at the urging of Frank Smith.

And the follow-up story to Frank Smith is that when I got elected to the presidency of the union in 1970, Frank was also elected to financial secretary. Those were the two full-time positions in Local 1064. And the point is this, that if I had the right to select my financial secretary—if I had had that right—that would have been Frank Smith. It would have been Frank Smith without question. He was the person that I would most closely want to work with. I had a lot of confidence and faith in him. And I knew he was a very honest man, upright man. So it was never any problem. None existed. 'Cause Frank never saw colour. He never saw religion. All he saw was a human being.

There's not very many people like that. We all have our prejudices to some extent. Frank was a man completely above that. He abhorred that sort of thing. And was quick to speak out against it—fearless, forceful, truthful, honest.

And there were others like him—Jim Ryan, who was the former president before I was, was also of the same ilk—interested in it from an early age. Jim Ryan was president of the local on a couple of occasions. He was a very good president—very able man. Again—fearless, straightforward, honest, very knowledgeable about the union and about the collective agreement. There was nobody, nobody that was the equal of Jim Ryan concerning knowledge of the collective agreement. A lot of the clauses that are in the present collective agreement were authored by Jim Ryan—particularly with respect to seniority.

Able men. Cecil Palmer was the chairman of the General Yard Grievance Committee at the time I was elected. And he served in that position over 30 years. Successive years. Another able, fearless, thoughtful, honest individual.

I was fortunate to have had those people as teachers. And when I

Frank Smith, Jim Ryan, and Cecil Palmer

got on the General Yard Committee I saw how they acted. And their behaviour was exemplary. They believed in an honest day's work—hear me, what I'm saying—for an honest day's pay. Again, you can't say that about everybody. But they were in a position of leadership as far as the union was concerned. And they acted it out. There were no shortcuts. If you had legitimate rights, they would fight tooth and nail to see that you attained those rights. And that nobody denied you. And I mean that. By the same token, if you were not entitled to a job, don't come to them seeking their support at the expense of somebody else—you just wouldn't get it. I learned that from them.

When they were going in on a regular grievance meeting with the superintendent, I got a learning experience. Just sat back. And you listened. When they spoke up to the superintendent, like they were talking to me. They didn't go in there bowing their head down with their cap in their hand—there was nothing like that. They went in—Cecil was the chairman. Cecil had the agenda. Gene Connolly, you must have heard of him, he was the superintendent from my time. "Now, Gene, we've got a number of items today. Let's us get right to it. We don't want to be talking about the hockey game." Now, Gene was a man who was interested in hockey and sports and all that sort of thing. Cecil would cut him off right in midstream. He would set out the agenda—A, B, C, right down the list.

I was learning.... They made no bones, had no favourites—

race, colour, religion—none of those things entered into their consideration.

Many of the other Grievance Committees actually assisted and practiced racial discrimination and religious discrimination. [General Yard Grievance Committee] wouldn't support it.

These guys were guys that would bring up cases on the floor [of the union hall]. A lot of it sometimes was of a discriminatory nature—not necessarily of racial, it could be religion, you know, or nationality. They would never get any support from [the president] on it. Oh, he'd pay lip service to it at the meeting. But he would avoid a clash with the management personnel who were responsible for what's going on. He'd never deal with it. He'd find some way to avoid it, by making promises about "It won't happen no more," and they were talking to this man—it was just only a cover.

(*How many terms did that person serve as president?*) He served about three terms. (*The steelworkers put him back in three times?*) At least three times. He had a big following. (*What does that tell you?*) Well, it tells you that the steelworkers weren't paying as close attention to the politics of the union as they should have been.

I defeated him in 1970....

But anyhow, let's get back to the discrimination.

So, there was discrimination practiced on the plant—combination of management and men. In many cases the people who were working on the plant aided and abetted it. 'Cause it was known, for example, that the bricklayers would not take on people of different nationalities. They discriminated against blacks—blacks couldn't get a job—that is, to be a bricklayer. You could be a bricklayer helper. That's all. People of foreign extraction from Europe could not get a job with the bricklayers.

And there was no doubt about it, there were a couple of people, men that I knew—bricklayers. In order for them to overcome that discrimination, changed their names. For instance, there was one fellow named Joe Stokola. He just cut off the last part of it and called himself Joe Stock....

(*Your father wanted to be a bricklayer....*) Oh, yeah, but he's visible. He was a black man. They openly told you you can't get in the bricklayers. They didn't bite their tongue about it or pretend

204

otherwise. They told you openly that you can't get a job there....
(*Tell me honestly, Winston—I know you were young, I know you were looking for fun—but did you not have anger?*) Not at that time. 'Cause we had a job. Every white person on the plant wasn't a bricklayer or a carpenter or electrician or machinist. You know? So in that sense, I wasn't discriminated against—I had a job!...

But you see, there were those blacks who had become members of the various Grievance Committees on the plant, who started advocating for minority rights. Sam Beckles was one; he was on the Grievance Committee, a black man. And he was very prominent—a forceful man, and who would take up those kind of challenges, and bring them to the knowledge of the executive. He was one of the leading advocates.

So it started gradually after the war. You must remember, the union wasn't strong either. So, you by yourself can't do very much if you haven't got a vehicle to use. You've got to have people of good will who are heading up that union. What's the good of a union if it's practicing discrimination?

(*So you're not going to work every day, gritting your teeth.*) No. I was glad to have a job. It's a whole different atmosphere. I have a job, the same as everybody else.

You know, we weren't aspiring to be electricians. A lot of us wanted to get in the Electrical Department because we knew the work in the Electrical Department was easier. And they'd go over there perhaps and work for a while. And the first thing you know— if they kept you over 30 days, in those days, they somehow were forced to [keep you on]. So before those 30 days were up, they would send you back to the General Yard. Say they didn't need you any more....

In those days, they never used to put up applications. It was only after the union got strong, the union said, "From now on, if you want men in your department: no more nepotism. You're not going to be able to allow your department heads to make the selection. You're going to put applications up so everybody could apply." That was a union regulation that they forced on management. A lot of the foremen and supervisors, of course, resisted it. But once we had that principle accepted by top management, then the union job was to police it to make sure that they didn't discrimi-

nate. But they could find ways to do it, covertly, you know.... Sometimes they would make out an application pretty well tailor-made
to the guy they want. He's the only one that had the qualifications....

But the union became stronger after the war. And people like I
mentioned—Cecil Palmer and Jim Ryan and Frank Smith—fought
against these discriminatory tactics that were going on....

(*So the times did change.*) Of course it changed. You've got to
understand, too, in a time of economic downfall, you're not going
to get a lot of progress. Are you? Everybody is an individual; everybody's interested in self. That's human nature. So, if I don't have
a job, I'm not worrying whether you've got one or not. Am I?

(*Well, there are some people who are more self-sacrificing.
But not generally.*) You know, you can't expect that. That's not the
way society works. If the dominant race in society don't have employment, you think they're going to worry about minorities?...

(*Was there ever before a black president of the steelworkers
union?*) No. No, I was the first, and the only.

(*The majority of the people that voted for you—would they be
black?*) No! Geez, the blacks—if we had about 50 to 75 black people working on the plant, among 4000 people, that's all we had.

(*So first you ran a campaign to get elected to the Grievance Committee.*) I really didn't. They knew that I was running because they had
to put the notices up on the bulletin board—that these people are running for the General Yard Grievance—voting would be on such-and-
such a day. (*You didn't have to make speeches?*) No. They knew you
and that's it. You never had to make any speeches. You never had
to go before a body. They knew who I was, they knew I was running. And they made a decision. I didn't go openly and ask people
to support me or vote for me. That was their choice.

I ran for the Recording Secretary position on the Executive in
1964—that's a step above the Grievance Committee. I was elected
to that. I defeated about three or four other guys.

(*So when you say you ran, that means....*) I was nominated on
the floor of the union hall. That's where you had to go and get a
nomination made and seconded, so it was officially entered in the
minutes. It's not a fly-by-night thing. I had people who advocated
to support Winston. That sort of thing. People did that. But they

The Rucks: Kenny, Marlene, Hazel (Roett), Winston, and Joyce

did that solely on their own. I had no organized campaign.

I always felt good about that. I didn't purposely sell or go around house-to-house. I had more pride in myself not to demean myself in that fashion.

I was elected Recording Secretary and I served there about three years. Regular meetings were held every week. My job was to record the minutes properly. And read the minutes. And read the correspondence. That sort of thing. Standard.

(*Why would you want a job like that?*) Well, it was an opportunity to me. And I particularly didn't seek it out by myself. I did it at the urging of people who figured that I would make a good executive officer, I suppose. To be frank about it. (*Did it relieve you of any work time?*) No. I had my job in the plant. (*So this is extra.*) Yes.

(*Maybe before we leave the Grievance Committee, I want to ask you: Did you, individually, actually do grievance fighting for people?*) Of course I did. That's my job. But I did it in conjunction with these other members of the Grievance Committee. I didn't do it alone. We never operated alone. That was a principle. Two men must go in and deal with any issue. There must be two of you. So that would prevent shysters from going in making deals with the superintendent or the assistant superintendent or the general foreman. It had to be two people, and it had to be recorded. You went in as official meeting. And you've got to report what you did when you went in there.

We go in and we meet with the superintendent, or the assistant superintendent, very often, who did most of the detailed work. And we'd go in in a formal manner. We'd have the seniority list to back us up. We're not going in there cold; we're going in there with information to support our contention. 'Cause you had to do your homework....

This is contract. This is collective agreement stuff. We refer to the section that that applies to in the collective agreement.

(*The Grievance Committee was nice training.*) Oh, the very best. The very best. And it gave you an air of self-confidence. And it gave you knowlege. You understand the workings of that collective agreement. You had to learn that; you had to know that. You had to, yourself, because you didn't always have the senior people there with you. And if you were in doubt, you go to them and get their understanding of it.

'Cause the clauses of the collective agreement sometimes are complex. It's not that simple. And it could be misread and misconstrued, and construed to use it different [for different] individuals. So that was fundamental. Anybody who wanted to be a good grievance man had to learn the collective agreement. And know what he was talking about. Know why that clause went in there. So once you knew that, nobody could trick you....

(*So now, the next role that you took on....*) I served on the vice-presidency. Martin Merner was president during that time. And I served in that capacity for three years, filling in occasionally, acquiring more knowledge, the inner workings then of the office, of the union. I became much more knowledgeable and more forceful, because I knew what I was dealing with from within our own union, because of the weaknesses that were there at the top....

(*How did you keep yourself separate from the president?*) Well, I would take an independent position on the floor of the hall. I told them how I felt about matters. They knew. You can't fool people forever. I was independent. And he knew that I was aspiring somehow, that people were supporting me. [Merner] was aware of that. And he used to do everything that he possibly could to try to put the knock on me. Not face-to-face; he would never deal with me face on to any issue. Because I was fearless. And I knew I knew more than him. Despite the fact that he had been there umpteen years, he had no more knowledge of that collective agreement than somebody who just got elected to the Grievance Committee. Because he didn't take any interest into it.

(*It's interesting: you can be his vice-president, but you're not expected to be loyal to the president.*) No, no—I'm loyal to the union.

I got elected vice-president, not with any luck of his own. I got elected vice-president in spite of him....

Anyhow, that's personalities....

And then coming 1970—people were urging me to run for the presidency. "You'll beat him. You'll beat him. No doubt about it." And I suppose anybody else could have beat him at that time 'cause he was ready to be defeated, I suppose. I just happened to come along at the right time, and I did defeat him. By a large majority.... Decisive.

(*Again, no election speeches?*) No. Just as long as my name stands. Somebody nominated me; they nominated him from the floor. All my speeches were made during those intervening years. Speeches pertaining to issues. But you were never expected to get up and say, "Well, I promise you this and I promise...." That was a lot of BS—nobody did that.... It wouldn't make sense. You never made [campaign] speeches. That was outlawed.

When you got elected, then you announced what you hoped to be part of your overall program, in conjunction with the other executive members. 'Cause it was a team.... That was the theory.

(*Did the press pick up the issue that there was a chance now a black man was going to become the leader of the union?*) No, no. No, it never became part of it. (*And among the union members, surely to God there were some who weren't happy with a black man.*) Oh, yes. Of course there were. [Merner] got a sizeable amount of votes....

(*By the time that you were running for president, did we have black men working on the railway?*) No, no. (*In the Electrical Office?*) Yes. I broke—myself, personally—I don't like to use the word "I." But as a result of being on the Grievance Committee and being on the Executive, I would take up cases where there was a general complaint of discrimination, constantly. I was not afraid to do that. I knew I had the backing of the union, overall—not in every case was I going to get support.

I'll give you an example. During the course of Jim Ryan's tenure as presidency—as I said, I was working in the General Yard. Jim Ryan was president between '64 and '67. So it was during that period I'm speaking about. The Open Hearth Department practiced discrimination on the furnaces. That is, a black man could not get a job working on the furnace, per se. Working on what they called the "bull gang." That bull gang were people who would fill positions on the furnace as First Helper and Second Helper. And that was a top job. Made big money, 'cause you got tonnage. So the bull gang was their source of replacement for job openings within the furnace itself. That was a hierarchy job, an elite job. It wasn't necessarily confined to religion. There were both Protestants and Catholics working on that job. Although the Open Hearth itself was considered a bastion of Roman papacy! *Winston laughs.*

So, this day in question I was sent down from the General Yard on a loan sheet, for work in the Open Hearth. I got down there. I was the senior man on the top of the list—the most seniority of that group— say it was 10 people. I went down. The loan sheet was given to Harry Martell, the labour supervisor that day. Harry is still talking about that today, because I talk to him frequently. So Harry took the loan sheet. I'm the top of the list, now. So, Harry started selecting people to go in various jobs. I knew all these jobs, and I knew the rate of money they paid. You understand.

"Well," he said—three fellows—they're all white and I was the only black man.... This is a top job. Top job.

So I was left there with two or three other fellows. And he said to me, "You fellows get shovels and come on with me."

I said, "Harry." So I sat down. I said, "Harry, where are we going?" "Oh," he said, "we're going to clean up something." I said, "Wait a minute, Harry." I said, "Not today. Not today." I said, "I'm top man. I'm the senior [over] all those other people. I have a right," I said, "to the job."

So he said, "Okay, wait here." Took the other guys, and left me there by myself. Gone for about, I would say close to a half hour. I sat back, there in the shack by myself, like this. And finally he came back. He said, "Okay, Winston. I was up from the floor, and I saw Jake." Jake was the general foreman in the Open Hearth that morning—big job. And Jake knew me well. Jake used to work side by side with me.

"I spoke to Jake," he said, "and to tell you to come on up on the furnace." I said, "Good." I grabbed my lunch bag, and I went up to the furnace. And when I got there, I saw Jake. He said, "Hi, Winston, how're you doing?" He said, "Go on Number 4 furnace." I said, "Okay, Jake."

I went and worked on Number 4 furnace with a fellow by the name of Angus MacDonald. He's since passed on. And I worked there with Angus that day. Angus treated me fine. I had no problem with Angus.

But it was like as if something big was happening. Because everybody started looking in my direction. The other guys who were working on the other furnaces—they were fairly close by— they saw this change and they knew this is something new that's happening today.

Now, mind you, I had a couple of good friends who were also on the furnace that day. And they were saying, "Well, if this was another turn—like say the 4 o'clock shift, or the backshift—then the guys would have walked off the job...."

But I knew that if this case would have gone any further—Jim Ryan was the president. Had this case gone any further—had the men walked off the job for example, or gone up to the union hall— I knew the kind of tongue-lashing they would have got from Jim Ryan over that situation. Now, they might have walked off the job— I'm not saying they wouldn't have—but they weren't going to get any support from him. He was not going to uphold it. And management was not going to challenge it at that point, you know. Because they knew I was within my rights.

So I worked that day, to make a long story short. The sun didn't fall out of the sky. You know. The furnace tapped out that day! They got a good heat! My blackness didn't make any change in the operation of the Open Hearth Department that day. And people would come up to me and congratulate me and say, "Winston, you broke in

there—you're the first black person that ever...." There were a lot of black people working around the different jobs there. They had to come to see to believe it. They had to come to see to believe it.

That was a big, big thing that day; it became public knowledge within the Open Hearth Department and in other parts of the Steel Plant. I didn't make no big deal about it. It was just another day's work, as far as I was concerned.... You can't stop change forever.

I think a lot of it depends, too, on the individual. I was always well-respected. Always well-respected. My whole family was. My father before me was a well-respected man. Had great influence within the community—the total community, not just the black community— the total community. So, you know, to that extent, people knew you and liked you. And I suppose that would make it kind of difficult for them to want to do anything to hurt you. Face on, that is.

I never ran into anybody that ever challenged me when I got the job, president of the local union, that came up to me and said, "You are a black fellow and you shouldn't be here." There were people that resented it, that you alluded to earlier on. And sometimes they would avoid me. Rather than come in and talk to me about a particular problem, they would go in and see Frank Smith. And Frank would send them over to see me. "Deal with Winston on that."

A Brief Chronology
of Cape Breton Steel

1880 Nova Scotia Steel & Coal Company (SCOTIA) builds a steel plant at New Glasgow and pours the first steel ingots in Canada at Ferrona.

1893 SCOTIA acquires the Wabana Iron Ore Mines, Newfoundland. Henry Melville Whitney is president of Dominion Coal Company (DOMCO), established to consolidate most coal mines in Cape Breton.

1899 Having failed to merge with SCOTIA, a Whitney-led consortium incorporates the Dominion Iron & Steel Company (DISCO) and buys from SCOTIA half the rights to Wabana Iron Ore Mines at Bell Island, Newfoundland. SCOTIA then buys the General Mining Association coal fields and transfers its basic steelmaking operations to Sydney Mines.

1900 Construction of the SCOTIA steel plant begins at Sydney Mines, to supply its finishing mills at New Glasgow. Construction by DISCO begins on a basic iron and steel plant in Sydney. Both plants will use Wabana ore. By December, skilled steelworkers strike.

1901 First steel is produced at Sydney on December 31.

1902 First steel produced at Sydney Mines.

1903 Strike at DISCO after company forces wage reductions. Machine Shop and Foundry added to Sydney plant.

1904 Provincial Workmen's Association (PWA) organizes a strike in 1904.

Views from the Steel Plant

Company wins, cutting wages and eliminating the union. This slows construction of the finishing mills, but the Rod Mill goes into operation.

1905   Rail Mill goes into production.

1907   Plagued by the high silicon and phosphorus content of Wabana ore, and the high sulfur content of Cape Breton coal, DISCO has difficulties producing steel economically. DISCO buys two Bessemer converters and experiments with combinations of Bessemer conversion processes and open hearth furnaces until World War One.

1910   Wire and Nail Mills are constructed.

1911   New Coke Ovens.

1912   DISCO adds a fifth blast furnace.

1913   Two 500-ton mixer furnaces are added.

1914   The first part of World War One (1914-1918) is a boom time that sees both plants at maximum operation. SCOTIA secures an order from the British Munitions Board for shell steel. DISCO's Rail Mill is equipped to roll shell rounds, and a deal with Peck Rolling Mills processes shell blanks from Sydney billets in Montreal. DISCO constructs a Plate Mill, but the end of the war reduces steel demand and the Plate Mill is mothballed, unused, until World War Two.

1918-19   Coke Ovens replaced by two 60-oven batteries.

1920   A consortium headed by Roy Wolvin creates Canada's largest corporate merger when British Empire Steel & Coal Company (BESCO) buys the DISCO and SCOTIA operations, including all the Wabana iron mines, most of the coal mines in Nova Scotia, and the Halifax Shipyards. Heavily over-capitalized, it sells shares for more than the operations are worth and pays out more dividends than the corporation can afford. Wage reductions lead to major strikes in the coal fields. Lack of capital means few plant improvements or renovations in steel.

1921   Undercapitalized BESCO closes the Sydney Mines steel plant. A third Coke Oven battery is added in Sydney. The Sydney operation supplies the car and axle shops at New Glasgow.

1922   Hours and wages are cut resulting in violent strikes and walk-outs.

1923   Another steel strike to establish a union leads to provincial police and the military being called in to aid civil power. Coal miners strike in sympathy, leading to the imprisonment of J. B. McLachlan and Dan Livingstone. John L. Lewis (international president of the United Mine Workers of America) revokes the charter, puts in his choice of union officials, and sends the coal miners back to work. The steel strike collapses. A company union is established, called the "Bischoff Plan."

1925   Long, bitter strike in coal.

1927   BESCO goes into bankruptcy. Receivers spend on improvements. A "flushing practice" that removes slag and silicon increases output and improves the quality of the steel.

1928-29   Steel Plant is operating at high capacity, making large profits. Dominion Steel & Coal Corporation (DOSCO) is formed in 1928. This is part of a large British conglomerate that takes over all of BESCO's assets. Also, the

A Brief Chronology of Cape Breton Steel

federal government grants Maritime freight rate subsidies.

1931 The Mackie Retarded Coolant Process is introduced. This gives DOSCO an advantage over rail producers and allows the Sydney plant to produce the world's finest rails. DOSCO holds the patent through the Mackie family. A completely integrated hospital is opened on DOSCO property. Time missed for medical reasons is drastically reduced and compensation payments are significantly reduced.

1937 Steelworkers spearhead the drive for public support leading to passage of the Trade Union Act, which gave the right to organize a union. Also, a 10-ton electric arc furnace for specialty steel is installed.

1938 Steelworkers are allowed to conduct a vote on steel plant property for the first time. The result is the formation of Local 1064, United Steelworkers of America.

1939 World War Two (1939-1945) leads to a boom period that lasts for the next 20 years. Women replace steelworkers lost to military service. Federal funding goes to Canada's major steel companies, but C. D. Howe (Minister of Munitions & Supply—nicknamed "Minister of Everything") is predisposed to channel investment to Ontario.

1940 The first contract is signed between the union and company. Number 2 Open Hearth Shop begins operation with two 200-ton tilting furnaces, and will eventually expand to six furnaces.

1941 German submarines sink four ships carrying DOSCO ore. Seventy lives are lost. The government agrees to renovate the Plate Mill mothballed in 1919.

1943 A national steel strike wins a small increase in the basic wage. New equipment includes Number 3 blast furnace, crushing and screening plant, and sintering plant.

1944 New 700-ton mixer installed.

Views from the Steel Plant

1945 Plate Mill is closed down due to lack of markets.

1947 Strike. At this time DOSCO negotiates as part of the Big Three: STELCO, ALGOMA, and DOSCO. This strike marks the end of this parity relationship. A new blast furnace is completed. DOSCO begins firing the open hearth furnaces with Bunker C oil instead of producer gas.

1949 Business across Canada booms. Sydney does not modernize as rapidly as its competitors. DOSCO expands its finishing mills in central Canada. There are 5400 employees in the Sydney plant. New Coke Ovens battery starts up.

1953 Another new Coke Ovens battery goes into operation. Blooming Mill is modernized.

1957 A. V. Roe Canada (Hawker-Siddeley) takes control of the plant. Over the next 10 years, closures include the Wire Mill, Nail Mill, Rod Mill, and Bar Mill. In June 1957, DOSCO adds a 225-ton open hearth furnace—a crucial technological miscalculation. DOSCO claims it uses the most up-to-date methods; but other steel plants install the Basic Oxygen Furnace (BOF).

1961 Slump in world steel market. Work force at plant drops to 2780, and never again reaches the 1950s numbers.

1966 New dock unloaders are constructed.

1967 Black Friday. Hawker-Siddeley announces the closure of the Steel Plant. A massive parade of concern by the community convinces the provincial government to take over the plant.

1968 The Steel Plant becomes a crown corporation and is now known as the Sydney Steel Corporation (SYSCO). Under R. B. Cameron, the plant makes money. Government announces plans for a 50-million-dollar expansion.

1969 SYSCO produces over one million tons of steel for the first time in history. The plant shows a profit and the employees receive their first and only bonus.

1970 Province announces 92-million-dollar modernization plan. It includes a modern rail finishing mill and a continuous caster. Instead of building BOF facilities, SYSCO invests in "submerged injection process" (SIP), invented in Sydney and not successful.

1972 Strike. Wages are the main issue. Settled by compromise.

1973 Steel plant is back into a bust cycle. A steel loader is constructed at the docks.

1974 Plans for a huge new basic steel complex to be constructed at Gabarus. Modernization at Sydney goes on hold. Cansteel plans cancelled during world slump in steel, 1975-77. SIDBEC-DOSCO installed electric arc furnace at Contrecoeur, Quebec—ending the purchase of billets or blooms from Sysco.

1975 The continuous caster is commissioned.

1980 The operation of the continuous caster is discontinued. The Rod and Bar Mills and Wire and Nail Mills are closed down during the 1970s. By the late 1970s, SYSCO's only finished product is rails.

1979 Plant reduced to one Blast Furnace, about 800 men laid off.

1980 Continuous caster goes into disuse. Many temporary layoffs.

A Brief Chronology of Cape Breton Steel

1981 Another modernization begins in two phases and will total 92 million dollars. Phase One includes a new blast furnace and rebuilding one coke ovens battery. Phase Two to include BOF or electric arc furnace and modern rail roll-

ing facilities. The south arm of Sydney Harbour is found to be heavily contaminated with industrial pollutants, prompting closure of commercial lobster fishery there.

1982 Strike. Workers leave the job prematurely not knowing the bad shape SYSCO is in: 3300 walk out; only 1200 return.

1985 Announcement of federal grant of 40 million dollars to clean up the Sydney Tar Ponds. A new agreement on Phase Two of modernization. Health and Welfare Canada says that Sydney residents suffered "significantly elevated mortality" from cancer. Another federal report warns re health risks of restarting the Coke Ovens. Province restarts the ovens.

1986 Future of plant again in doubt. Another "Save SYSCO" campaign.

1987 Second phase of modernization begins. The plant becomes a mini-mill with an electric arc furnace feeding a bloom caster and a universal Rolling Mill.

1988 Strike in February. Union removes "maintenance" personnel. Coke Ovens permanently shut down early. Each side blames the other.

1989 Blast Furnace and Open Hearth shut down.

1990 Provincial government writes off 785 million dollars of debt. Says plant must show a profit to continue operating and seek a buyer.

1993 MinMetals of China agrees to purchase the steel plant after operating it as a joint venture with the provincial government for three years.

1995 Maximum employment is now only 600. Steel production is good, but 203 million dollars more debt accumulates.

1996 MinMetals withdraws from its agreement with the government.

1997 Government seeks another buyer.

2000 On May 22nd, the last steel is produced. With no purchaser for the plant, the Nova Scotia government closes SYSCO permanently.

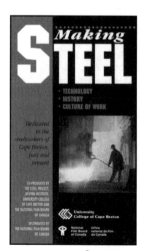

Available from **Breton Books**

See the Sydney Steel Plant in action in this exciting, full-colour video. **Making Steel** offers extraordinary, never-to-be-seen-again shots of the Blast Furnace, cutting steel, the Coke Ovens—process after process. Part 1, **Technology**, captures the enormous complexity and awesome beauty of steelmaking. Part 2, **History**, moves from the boom years through to new technologies for recycling steel. And in **Culture of Work**, steelworkers talk of camaraderie, danger, pride in workmanship, and community.

The Steel Project and National Film Board of Canada.

60-minute video **$30.00** includes tax & shipping

ORDER NOW FROM:

Breton Books

Wreck Cove, Cape Breton, Nova Scotia B0C 1H0
bretonbooks@ns.sympatico.ca • 1-800-565-5140

SEE OUR COMPLETE CATALOGUE AT **www.capebretonbooks.com**